CALL CENTER FORECASTING AND SCHEDULING:

The Best of
Call Center Management Review

Call Center Press™

A Division of ICMI, Inc.

Published by:
Call Center Press
A Division of ICMI, Inc.
P.O. Box 6177
Annapolis, Maryland 21401 USA

Design by Ellen K. Herndon

Printed in the United States of America

Library of Congress Catalog Card Number:

ISBN 0-9659093-6-0

Table of Contents

Foreword

These are exciting times for call center managers. As call centers transition from telephone-centric support operations to multi-channel communications powerhouses, they are increasingly recognized for their central role in cultivating and maintaining customer loyalty. And call center management—once in the category of "mystical arts"—is one of today's hottest professions.

But managing a call center requires specialized knowledge and skills – you can't just "wing it!" Successful call center management depends on "getting the right people and supporting resources in place at the right times to handle an accurately forecasted workload, at service level and with quality." There is simply no way to establish and operate an effective environment without a solid understanding of the principles behind forecasting, staffing, scheduling, service level, queuing dynamics, and real-time management.

The articles in this collection focus squarely on these vital topics. Originally published in the pages of *Call Center Management Review* (formerly *Service Level Newsletter*), they were selected for their educational value, practicality, and most importantly, coverage of timeless call center management principles.

We hope you enjoy the book!

Sincerely,

The *Call Center Management Review* Team

Chapter 1:
Establishing Service Level Objectives

Service Level and Response Time in a New Era (Part 1)

Service Level and Response Time in a New Era (Part 2)

Abandonment: Not the Best Measure of Call Center Performance

Service Level and Response Time in a New Era (Part 1)

by Brad Cleveland

Service level is at the heart of effective incoming call center management. Resource planning has long been based on achieving a specified service level objective, which takes the form: "X percent of all calls will be answered in Y seconds." Without a concrete objective, you will not be able to meet or exceed your customers' expectations. And the answers to many important questions would be left to chance, such as: How accessible is your call center? What is the optimum level of staff and supporting resources? How do you compare to others? Are you prepared to handle the response to marketing campaigns? How busy are your reps going to be? What are your costs going to be?

Service level is tried and true in call centers worldwide for transactions that must be handled when they arrive. Inbound phone calls are the most common example today. New multimedia services such as video calls and calls integrated with the World Wide Web also fit into this category. Consequently, service level will remain an important objective in the next generation of call centers.

Most call centers are also responsible for transactions that belong in a second category – those that don't have to be handled at the time they arrive. Examples include correspondence, e-mail, faxes, walk-in traffic, voicemail and videomail. These transactions allow a larger window of time in which the call center can

> **TWO MAJOR CATEGORIES OF INBOUND TRANSACTIONS**
>
> 1. Those that must be handled when they arrive (i.e., inbound calls). Performance objective: Service Level.
> 2. Those that can be handled at a later time (i.e., correspondence). Performance objective: Response Time.

respond. But it is becoming increasingly important for call centers to: 1) establish concrete "response time" objectives for these contacts, and 2) ensure that the objectives are met through disciplined resource planning and management.

Choosing and achieving both service level and response-time objectives are, in many ways, similar. But there are also important differences.

THE LINK BETWEEN RESOURCES AND RESULTS

A concrete service level objective provides the necessary link between the on-phone staff required and the results you will achieve. For example, imagine you are going to receive 50 calls that last an average of three minutes in a half-hour period. If you have only two people to answer the calls, the delay time for most callers will be long, and you'll probably have high abandonment. As you add people, delay times will drop. How many people should you add? Enough to reduce the queue to an acceptable level for you and your callers. In other words, the answer is your service level target, and you won't be able to achieve it without the correct level of resources.

The same principle is true for transactions that don't have to be handled when they arrive. A clear, agreed-upon objective provides the necessary link between the resources you need and the response time you want to achieve. And choosing a service level for either type of transaction involves considering many of the same questions. For example, how motivated are customers to reach you? What are their expectations? How much time do customers have to wait for a reply? What level of service is your competition providing? How about those who are "best in class"?

If response time is bad enough, what started out as a fax or e-mail can turn into a phone call.

On the other hand, the methods used to calculate resources for the two categories of transactions are very different. For transactions that must be handled when they arrive, the queuing formula Erlang C or a computer simulation program that takes random call arrival into account is generally used to calculate on-phone staff.

For the second category of transactions, required staff can be calculated by the conventional industrial planning method of dividing units of projected work by an average productivity figure. For example, if there are 50 letters to respond to, and reps can process an average 10 in an hour, the equivalent of five rep-hours are required. Staffing requirements for these activities are then added as an additional tier to the staffing requirements for handling calls. Within feasible response-time parameters, these activities are scheduled into periods when the call load is relatively light.

SERVICE LEVEL WITH QUALITY

A poor service level feeds on itself. As service deteriorates, more and more callers are likely to verbalize their criticisms when their calls are finally answered. Reps spend valuable time apologizing to callers, which drives up average handling time. And that means they are not be able to handle as many calls as they could if service was better. Furthermore, they will eventually pace themselves differently. If they can't get a "breather" between calls because the "in-between" time no longer exists, they may start taking their breathers while they're on calls as a survival mechanism. Turnover and burnout may go up, which will drive up recruitment and training costs.

Quality also tends to suffer, which has a cyclical, negative impact on service level. When reps are overworked because of long caller queues, they become less accurate, lose their powers of concentration and are generally less "customer friendly." They make more mistakes. These mistakes contribute to repeat calls, unnecessary service calls, escalation of calls and complaints to higher management, callbacks, etc. – all of which drive service level further down. In short, poor service level tends to be a vicious cycle.

The relationship between quality and response time is similar. For example, if customers don't receive a reply to an e-mail as quickly as expected, they may send another. This can be the start of a similar cycle. In addition, if response time is bad enough, what started out as a fax or e-mail can turn into a phone call: "I'm calling to check up on an e-mail I sent to you. I haven't heard a reply yet and I'm wondering…" And in most call centers, if the original transaction from the customer hasn't yet been handled, reps won't have the information necessary to deal with these calls without duplicating efforts for both the call center and caller.

MEASURING ACTIVITY

Reporting and management tools for transactions that must be handled when they arrive are excellent. Modern call center systems provide a wealth of user-specified, detailed information. Unfortunately, that is generally not the case for transactions that can be handled later. Even high-end forecasting and scheduling software programs do not yet seamlessly factor these activities into the planning process. You can input them manually, but that assumes you are able to measure them and know what to enter.

This is a challenge that systems and software providers are working on, and a variety of solutions are in the pipeline. But in the meantime, call center managers often need to piece together disparate reports.

TIME TO GET CREATIVE

Customers are demanding choices in how they are served, and call centers are finding new and creative ways to meet those demands. The result is that call centers have more types of transactions to handle. Service level is a well-established objective for transactions that must be handled when they arrive. Similarly, response time is an important objective for transactions that can be handled at a later time.

In Part 2 (on page 5), we'll pick up with how to measure and manage activities that require response-time objectives.

Service Level and Response Time in a New Era (Part 2)

by Brad Cleveland

Chapter 1

Customers are demanding choices in how they are served and call centers are finding new and creative ways to meet those demands. The result is that call centers have more types of transactions to handle, which must be planned for and managed appropriately.

As discussed in Part 1 of this series (see page 2), service level is a solid, common objective for transactions that must be handled when they arrive. Response time is the equivalent of service level for transactions that don't have to be handled when they arrive. Like service level, response time provides the critical link between the resources you need and the results you want to achieve.

EXAMPLE OBJECTIVES

Choosing response time objectives involves considering many of the same questions you analyzed when choosing an appropriate service level (i.e., the factors affecting tolerance, see box page 6). Examples of typical response time objectives include:

TYPE OF TRANSACTION	LOW END OF RANGE	HIGH END OF RANGE
Customer E-mail	Three days	Within one hour
Fax	Three days	Three hours
Voicemail	Next day	Within one hour
Letter by mail	One week	Same day

Studies on this subject are confirming that customer expectations are rising, and we expect that organizations will continue to boost these objectives.

RELAYING OBJECTIVES TO CUSTOMERS

An important step in establishing response time objectives is one not usually associated with service level: You need to relay to customers what your objectives are. That means telling them up front what they can expect (i.e., in literature, through the VRU, on your Web site, etc.). Otherwise, what started out as a fax or e-mail may turn into a phone call: "I'm calling to check up on an e-mail I sent to you. I haven't heard a reply yet and I'm wondering…"

Consultant Martin Prunty, a well-known expert on the future of call centers, says, "You have to be overt about it. Don't leave their expectations to chance or you'll pay the price." In most call centers, if the original transaction from the customer hasn't yet been handled, reps won't have the information necessary to deal with these calls without duplicating efforts for both the call center and the caller.

INTERNAL COMMUNICATIONS

Meeting response time objectives sometimes requires various internal resources to be available at the right times. For example, some incoming messages to help desks that arrive from the Web or by fax require reps to confer with an "internal help desk" or another agent group. Consequently, you must also establish "internal response time" standards.

At the very least, workgroups need an agreement that specifies how and when individuals will interact with each other. The agreement should stipulate levels of priorities and appropriate responses for each.

For example, e-mail priorities are sometimes categorized as follows:

1. Urgent messages. Recipients are expected to respond as soon as they get the message. This would be appropriate for customer-driven activities where a quick response time is important. Most voicemail and virtually all e-mail systems allow the sender to designate whether the message is a priority.

2. Routine messages. Recipients are expected to respond within, say, four hours or one day.

3. Informational messages. These messages require no response.

Internal e-mail messages should have descriptive titles and be written like a newspaper story, with headlines first, the main points second and necessary supporting details last. Many of the same principles apply to internal phone calls, faxes and voicemail. For example, voicemail messages should begin with a brief introduction to the subject and the level of priority it should receive.

A useful way to identify the resources required to handle a transaction is to create a step-by-step flow chart of the process. You should begin by charting processes as they now exist and then develop a new chart of the "ideal." This will identify weak links in the processes and reveal where internal standards are necessary.

FACTORS AFFECTING CUSTOMER TOLERANCE

- Degree of Motivation
- Availability of Substitutes
- Competition's Response Time
- Level of Expectations
- Time Available
- Who's Paying for the Transaction?
- Human Behavior

FORECASTING

As with inbound transactions that must be handled when they arrive, the volumes and average handling times of other transactions almost always occur in predictable, repeating patterns. They also often correlate to other forecasts, such as the inbound call load, units of sales or number of customers.

Consequently, many of the same general principles used to forecast call load apply:

- Identify repeating patterns by month of year, day of week and time of day.
- Choose an increment of time sufficient to calculate base staff requirements.
- Break the patterns down into proportions, and use the proportions to project future traffic.

- Blend the appropriate amount of judgment into the forecast (i.e., what is the marketing department about to do that will impact volume and type of transactions you receive?).

STAFFING/SCHEDULING

The methods you will use for calculating base staff are very different for the two types of transactions. For transactions that must be handled when they arrive, either the queuing formula Erlang C or a computer simulation program that takes random call arrival into account is used to calculate on-phone staff.

However, to calculate the staff required for transactions that do not have to be handled when they arrive, you can usually get adequate results with more traditional methods of industrial planning. For example, if you have 50 customer e-mail messages to respond to that require an average of three minutes processing time, there is 50 x 3, or 150 minutes of workload to handle. Since there are 60 minutes in an hour, the work will require 150/60, or 2.5 base staff hours. That's assuming 100 percent efficiency (which is not realistic), so you will need to adjust base staffing estimates upward. You also need to consider inaccuracies in staffing and plan for a margin of error.

(Note, some traffic engineers recommend using Erlang C when response time objectives are less than an hour. The assumptions of Erlang C are valid because the work arrives randomly and is "queued" until handled.)

The response time objectives you establish will dictate when this work must be scheduled. For example, if you promise a next-day response, you'll need to forecast the transactions for a day and ensure that enough staff are scheduled to handle the work within 24 hours. If you promise a one-hour response, you'll need to schedule enough staff to handle the transactions that arrive each hour, within the next hour. You'll also need to factor in necessary breaks and other activities.

CONCLUSION

Like service level, response time is the necessary mechanism for "getting the right people in the right places at the right times" so that you are meeting your customers' expectations. Achieving response time objectives requires many of the same planning steps necessary to achieve service level objectives:

- Set response time objectives.
- Forecast these transactions, within timeframes specific enough to calculate base staff required.
- Calculate base staff required to meet your objectives.
- Account for breaks, absenteeism and other factors that will keep your agents from the work.
- Organize schedules around overall staffing needs.

Abandonment: Not the Best Measure of Call Center Performance

by Brad Cleveland

Call center managers often ask the questions: What is an acceptable rate of abandonment? What is abandonment in my industry? Are there any studies on how long callers will wait? What should our service level be to keep abandonment under X percent?

The usual assumptions are that there must be industry "standards" for abandonment, and that abandonment is a good indicator of call center performance. Consider, though, the following realities.

IT IS DIFFICULT TO ACCURATELY FORECAST ABANDONMENT

To understand abandonment — why, when and how much — it is necessary to understand caller tolerance. There are seven factors that affect caller tolerance (see Figure 1):

1. Degree of motivation. How important is the call to them? What are the consequences to them of not getting through? How badly do they need or want the product or service? Or to provide or receive information? Callers to airlines wait longer during "super-saver" promotions than at other times. Callers with power-outages will wait longer to reach their utility than those with billing questions.

Figure 1

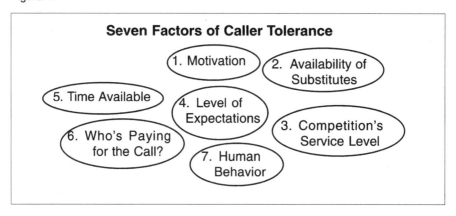

Seven Factors of Caller Tolerance

1. Motivation
2. Availability of Substitutes
5. Time Available
4. Level of Expectations
3. Competition's Service Level
6. Who's Paying for the Call?
7. Human Behavior

2. Availability of substitutes. Even though they are highly motivated to make the call, callers who encounter difficulties may abandon if they know of another way to satisfy their need. Fax, mail, automated alternatives, competitors and "reading the manual" are all examples of potential substitutes. If callers are highly motivated and have no substitutes, they will retry many times if they get busies, and will generally wait a very long time in queue. Even though they do not abandon, they still might be very unhappy about the experience.

3. Competition's service level. Traditional competitors have an influence, but a call center is often its own competition. For example, if a primary queue backs up, callers may dial other numbers available, or they may choose incorrect routing selections in the VRU just to reach a rep... any rep, quicker (causing transferred calls, inflated reports and longer handling times).

4. Level of expectations. The experiences callers have had with the call center, and the reputation that the organization or industry has for service (or the level of service being promoted) have a direct bearing on tolerance.

5. Time available. How much time do callers have to accomplish the call? Doctors who call insurance providers have a well-deserved reputation for not tolerating even a modest wait (or what most of us would perceive to be a modest wait). Retirees calling the same companies may have time to chat.

6. Who's paying for the call? Callers are usually more tolerant when they are not paying for the call (e.g., using 800 service).

7. Human behavior. The weather, the caller's mood and the day's news all have some immeasurable bearing on caller tolerance.

These factors determine how many callers will abandon and when they will abandon — among other things, such as how many times callers will retry when encountering busies and how understanding they will be of any time spent waiting in queue. So the conditions causing lost calls are constantly changing and there are a lot of variables. To predict abandonment with consistent accuracy, we would have to know exactly how the previously mentioned factors are going to influence our callers in future periods of time.

Incidentally, there are forecasting and workforce management software programs that include lost call predictions. They generally require average time to abandonment as input, and will then use statistical techniques to distribute calls around the average to calculate approximately what percent of the calls would abandon within 5 seconds, 10 seconds, 15 seconds and so forth. They then work these percentages against the forecasted queue (based on a queuing formula), and calculate the predicted lost calls. But software can't predict the factors affecting caller tolerance and how they are going to shift, so the abandonment forecast is usually not very accurate.

ABANDONMENT CAN BE A MISLEADING MEASURE OF CALL CENTER PERFORMANCE

A popular and sometimes inaccurate assumption is that longer queues translate into higher abandonment. The seven factors can help to explain apparent paradoxes:

- When the stock market swings significantly, mutual funds and others in the financial industry tend to get a lot of unexpected calls. But even though service level may drop, abandonment also goes down because callers have a higher degree of motivation — and are willing to wait longer, if necessary.

Chapter 1

- When airlines run super-saver specials, callers are generally willing to wait longer. Service level may drop because of the heavy response from callers but abandonment also goes down.
- When storms cause power outages, abandonment is often low in utility call centers even though service level may be poor.
- If callers encounter a lot of busy signals before they get into the queue, they will almost always wait longer, if necessary. (They're thinking something like: "Geesh, at least I'm connected. I'd better hang in there.")

While these may be obvious examples, what about the more subtle day-by-day shifts in caller tolerance? It can be baffling. Sometimes, when people have to wait a long time, they wait. Other times, when service level is really good, abandonment is high. If you don't believe it, graph out service level vs. abandonment by the half-hour for a few typical days. You're not likely to see an exact correlation.

Call centers with low service levels don't recognize a problem because abandonment is low (and they usually aren't bothering to ask callers what they think).

THE CALL CENTER
CANNOT DIRECTLY CONTROL ABANDONMENT

The previous examples notwithstanding, abandonment generally goes down if we answer calls faster (improve service level). If there is no queue, there would be no opportunity for callers to abandon — so, some managers reason, don't have a queue!

However, for most call centers, answering all calls immediately would be a highly impractical goal. The reason, of course, is the law of diminishing returns applied to call center staffing: "When successive individual telephone reps are assigned to a given call load, marginal improvements in service level that can be attributed to each additional rep will eventually decline." The table in Figure 2 illustrates this reality. So most call centers have a queue at least part of the time. And any time there is a queue, there is opportunity for callers to abandon.

In the final analysis, we can control how accessible we are through: 1) How many trunks we have; and 2) how many

Figure 2

Reps	Percent of calls answered immediately
59	10%
60	24%
61	36%
62	47%
63	56%
64	64%
65	70%
66	76%
67	81%
68	85%
69	88%
70	91%
71	93%
72	94%
73	96%
74	97%
75	98%
76	98%
77	99%

Talk time: 180 sec.;
work time: 30 sec.; calls: 500

skilled reps are plugged in. But we can't control how callers will react or the myriad circumstances that influence their behavior.

Too many call center managers are being held accountable for abandonment, which is something they cannot directly control. It's much more equitable and productive to hold them accountable for things they can control, such as service level. And if the call center is hitting an appropriate service level objective, abandonments (and busies) are not generally a problem.

Chapter 2:
Forecasting the Workload

The Art of Counting Callers: Adjusting for Busies and Abandonments

by Brad Cleveland

In most incoming call centers, calls arrive in repeating patterns, typically by season of year, day of week and half-hour of day. Accordingly, "time-series" forecasting methodologies, which assume that past patterns will continue into the future, are popular with call center managers. When time series forecasts are blended with appropriate interdepartmental coordination and judgment, forecasts for the aggregate workload can be quite accurate, down to specific future periods of time.

But there's an important caveat to using historical data — it must accurately reflect the number of callers who attempted to reach you. If it ignores callers who got busy signals or who abandoned their calls, you will underestimate future calling demand. If it includes every busy signal and abandoned call, you will most likely overestimate demand.

FAR-REACHING CONSEQUENCES

Building your forecast on accurate data is critical. The forecast is the basis for determining staffing needs and requirements for other resources, such as how many workstations are required and how many trunks are necessary. It provides the foundation for:

- Calculating base staff required to meet your service level objectives.
- Calculating trunking and system requirements.
- Minimizing abandoned and blocked calls.
- Organizing accurate, workable schedules.
- Predicting future staffing and network costs.
- Meeting caller expectations.
- Creating an environment in which quality service can be provided.

If the forecast is not reasonably accurate, the rest of the planning process will be off the mark. Adjusting for busy signals and abandoned calls is an important prerequisite to utilizing historical data.

OFFERED CALLS VS. INDIVIDUALS

The historical data you use in forecasting should reflect "offered calls" discounted for multiple attempts from individual callers. Offered calls include all of the attempts your callers make to reach you. There are three possibilities for offered calls: they can get busy signals; they can be answered by the system but hang up before reaching a rep; or they can be answered by a rep. (See Figure 1, page 15)

There's been a lot of confusion around the term "offered call." Some define it as a call that reaches the ACD. Some ACDs use that definition and have a report labeled offered calls, which is the sum of answered calls (those that reach reps) and abandoned calls. However, the traditional definition of offered call — and the one I'll stick with here — is any attempt a caller makes to reach you, even if the call never reaches the ACD (i.e., they get a busy signal in the network). Your ACD reports don't necessarily have the complete picture.

Figure 1

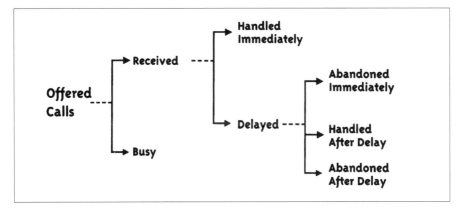

ABANDONED CALLS

Acquiring data on abandoned calls is easy. Virtually every ACD provides reports on abandonments down to the half-hour. The seven factors of caller tolerance will influence how long of a queue callers will tolerate, how many will abandon and how many will call back if they abandon. Most call center managers count abandoned calls "one for one." The usual logic is that the forecast is based on half-hour data and that callers who abandon are not likely to call back within the half-hour.

SEVEN FACTORS AFFECTING CALLER TOLERANCE:

1. Degree of Motivation
2. Availability of Substitutes
3. Competition's Service Level
4. Level of Expectations
5. Time Available
6. Who's Paying for the Call
7. Human Behavior

To the degree that callers who abandon call back and get through to agents, they will be counted more than once in the data. Consequently, some managers have used everything from educated guesses to hard data via automatic number identification (ANI) to discount a portion of the abandoned calls.

Without good data, you run the risk of discounting calls too deeply, which will lead to a forecast that underestimates demand. We generally recommend including all abandoned calls in the data, unless you have ANI reports that you can use as a guide. This may lead to a forecast that somewhat overstates demand; however, a forecast that underestimates demand will likely lead to insufficient staffing and abandoned calls, which will perpetuate the problem.

BUSY SIGNALS

Adjusting for busy signals can be a trickier challenge. The age-old question is, do 100 busy signals represent 100 people who tried to reach you once, or one persistent soul who tried 100 times? The answer is usually in between. Studies have shown that even when callers have other options, they will generally retry at least once or twice when they get a busy signal. So busy signals should almost always be discounted. The question is: How much?

SOURCES OF DATA

Callers will encounter busy signals either when you don't have enough physical capacity to handle the calls or when you've programmed your ACD system to reject calls from entering the queue if the wait backs up beyond a threshold you've defined. Consequently, data on busy signals may need to come from your ACD, local telephone company, long distance provider or all of the above.

Virtually all ACDs have a report called "all trunks busy" (ATB). This will tell you how much of the time and how many times all of the trunks in a specific group were 100 percent occupied. But it won't tell you how many attempts callers made to reach you when all trunks were busy, nor how many callers were represented by those attempts.

If you have an ACD that can dynamically generate busy signals based on real-time circumstances, it will generally provide a report on how many calls received busies. Likewise, you can obtain basic reports from your local and long-distance providers that give data on how many times busies were generated for specific time periods. However, these basic reports won't tell you how many individuals are represented by those attempts, unless you can capture callers' numbers and run a sort to identify multiple attempts.

Over the past years, long-distance companies have been providing more advanced reports that help to solve the retrial mystery. These reports provide actual retrial rates, down to specific increments of time that you specify.

Alternatives to actual retrial reports can include customer surveys, answering all calls for a short period (even if by voicemail) to determine true demand and variations of judgment (guessing). Naturally, it's best to have hard data. But whatever information is available, be sure to question the rules of thumb which state that callers will retry an average three to five times. Like abandonments, retries are determined by the seven factors affecting caller tolerance, and three to five attempts may be way off the mark for your callers.

Even if you are in a situation where you don't have the staffing resources you need to handle the load, your forecast should be as realistic as possible. That is a first step toward knowing what you can accomplish with the resources you have and securing the resources you need. Adjusting your data so that it accurately reflects the individuals attempting to reach you should be an ongoing part of the forecasting process.

Forecasting Calls (Part 1): Breaking Down Total Calls Demand

by Gordon Mac Pherson

"The future is really the composite outcome of such a multitude of factors that, beyond a certain level, the precise computations of the highly trained and expensively equipped add little over common sense and a more generalized approach..."

Daniel B. Nickell in Forecasting on Your Microcomputer
Tab Books Inc.

Forecasting calls means estimating, down to the half-hourly staff planning level, how many calls your incoming call center will be offered in a future time period. Forecasting calls is the first step in determining the workload your call center should be equipped to handle. (The second step is to know what your Average Talk Time and Average After Call Work Time are.) If you miss your forecast by a significant amount, everything else you do right could be for nothing.

Professional forecasters generally consider forecasts out to three months to be short-term; from three months to two years, medium-term; and further than two years, long-term. Most incoming call center forecasts cover a year because they are done to justify annual budget requests. But some forecasts cover as many as five or even 10 years, because estimated requirements for a new call center must be established. Other forecasts only predict how many calls to expect in the next half-hour, or the coming afternoon (intra-day forecasting). The basic principles and concepts are the same in every case.

There are two levels of activity in forecasting calls. At one level you determine the total number of calls you will receive; at another level you break the total down into its seasonal, monthly, weekly, daily and half-hourly components. Some call centers break the total down into 15-minute components.

Figure 1

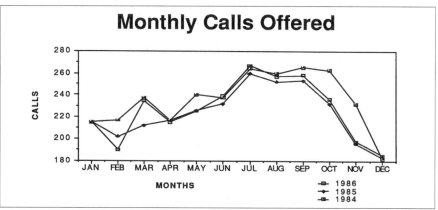

The factors which enable you to break demand down to its half-hourly components are derived by simple arithmetic and are relatively reliable. Calling patterns almost always exist, and they are detectable if you keep and analyze historical records. (See Figure 1 on page 17 and Figures 2 and 3 below.)

After you collect adequate data on the volume of calls offered in October, for example, you may discover that the percent or proportion of a year's calls which occur in that month is fairly constant. The same applies for the percent or proportion of a week's calls which occur on Mondays, or any other specific

Figure 2

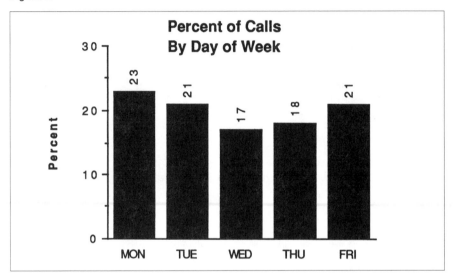

Figure 3

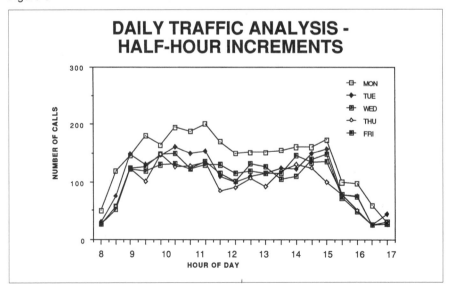

day of the week. And the same goes for different time periods during the day, such as 10 a.m. to 10:30 a.m., 10:30 a.m. to 11 a.m., and so forth. The trick is to have the data and see if the patterns repeat themselves. If they do, you've got something to use for forecasting. Examples of how such data is tracked and calculated are shown in Figures 4 and 5 below, and Figure 6 on page 20. Many incoming call centers use software to accomplish this.

Figure 4

Half-Hourly Calls Worksheet

| | Date ____ | | Date ____ | | Date ____ | | Date ____ | | Date ____ | | Av |
	Calls	Prop.	Calls	Prop.	Calls	Prop.	Calls	Prop.	Calls	Prop.	Pr
08:00 - 08:30											
08:30 - 09:00											
09:00 - 09:30											
09:30 - 10:00											
10:00 - 10:30											
10:30 - 11:00											
11:00 - 11:30											
11:30 - 12:00											
12:00 - 12:30											
12:30 - 13:00											
13:00 - 13:30											
13:30 - 14:00											
14:00 - 14:30											
14:30 - 15:00											
15:00 - 15:30											
15:30 - 16:00											
16:00 - 16:30											
16:30 - 17:00											
17:00 - 17:30											
17:30 - 18:00											
Total											

Instructions: To calculate proportions, divide calls for half hour by total for day.

Figure 5

Day of Week Calls Worksheet

Week of	Mon	Prop	Tue	Prop	Wed	Prop	Thu	Prop	Fri	Prop	Calls Total
Average											

Instructions:
1. Fill in "Week of" column with beginning date of week.
2. Fill in number of calls under each each day's heading.
3. At end of week, total calls and fill in under "Calls Total."
4. Divide each day's calls by "Call Total" for the week and fill in under "Prop."
5. To calculate averages, add all proportions on a per day of the week basis, and divide by number of entries in respective "Prop" column.

Chapter 2

Figure 6

Day of Month and Month of Year Calls Worksheet

YEAR _____

Summary

Day	Jan	Prop	. . .	Dec	Prop	Avg Prop	Total Calls
1	—	—		—	—	—	—
2	—	—		—	—	—	—
3	—	—		—	—	—	—
4	—	—		—	—	—	—
5	—	—		—	—	—	—
6	—	—		—	—	—	—
7	—	—		—	—	—	—
8	—	—		—	—	—	—
9	—	—		—	—	—	—
10	—	—		—	—	—	—
11	—	—		—	—	—	—
12	—	—		—	—	—	—
13	—	—		—	—	—	—
14	—	—		—	—	—	—
15	—	—		—	—	—	—
16	—	—		—	—	—	—
17	—	—		—	—	—	—
18	—	—		—	—	—	—
19	—	—		—	—	—	—
20	—	—		—	—	—	—
21	—	—		—	—	—	—
22	—	—		—	—	—	—
23	—	—		—	—	—	—
24	—	—		—	—	—	—
25	—	—		—	—	—	—
26	—	—		—	—	—	—
27	—	—		—	—	—	—
28	—	—		—	—	—	—
29	—	—		—	—	—	—
30	—	—		—	—	—	—
31	—	—		—	—	—	—
Total	—		. . .	—			—
Prop. of Year	—		. . .	—			

Instructions:

1. Fill in calls for each day of each month.
2. Calculate total calls for each month at end of month.
3. Divide each day's calls by total calls for that month to obtain proportion.
4. At end of year, add proportions for each day of month going across and divide by number of months. Number of months is usually 12, but varies because not every month has 31 days. Put answer in "Avg Prop" column.
5. At end of year, add calls for each day of month column going across. Put totals under "Total Calls."
6. At end of year, divide each month's total calls by year's total calls to obtain monthly proportions.

As an example of how to go from total demand down to any half-hour's worth of calls, suppose you are simply told (directed) to plan for 10 percent growth as compared to the current year. Assuming that you have been keeping the right records and that you have confidence in your data, you could estimate the calls you expect to receive in any particular half-hour through use of the following formula: [(Current Year's # of calls x 1. 10 x Month's Proportion of calls)/Number of Operations Days in Month] x Day of Week Index Factor x Half-Hour Proportion = Half-Hour's Calls. The results of such a calculation are shown in Figure 7 (below).

The problem with this example is that it assumes all Mondays are the same, all Tuesdays, all Wednesdays, etc. This is not always the case. In reality, weeks with call center holidays (closings) in them create a special problem. Some Tuesdays, for example, follow three-day holidays, and they are definitely not like ordinary Tuesdays. Obviously, the Day Of Week Index Factors will not be the same as they would be for a normal week. The solution, once again, is to identify historical patterns, and calculate a special set of Day Of Week Index Factors for weeks with holidays in them. (See Figure 8 on page 22.)

Figure 7

**Breaking Down A Total Forecast
To Its Half-Hourly Components**

500,000	Current year's calls
x 1.1	To add 10%
550,000	Estimated calls in forecast year
x .068	January proportion
37,400	January calls
÷ 21	Operations days - January
1,781	Average calls per day
x 1.125	Monday index factor
2,004	Monday's calls
x .055	10:00 - 10:30 proportion
110	forecasted calls 10:00 - 10:30

Notes:
1. To determine operations days, count (circle) the days call center will be open.
2. To calculate day of week index factor, divide day of week proportion by average day of week proportion.

	Prop.		Avg Prop.		Index Factor
Example:					
Monday	.225	÷	.2	=	1.125
Tuesday	.210	÷	.2	=	1.050
Wednesday	.170	÷	.2	=	0.850
Thursday	.180	÷	.2	=	0.900
Friday	.215	÷	.2	=	1.075

JANUARY 1991

S	M	T	W	T	F	S
		1	2	3	4	5
6	7	8	9	10	11	12
13	14	15	16	17	18	19
20	21	22	23	24	25	26
27	28	29	30	31		

Another problem is that calling patterns are sometimes affected by regularly scheduled events such as paydays, billing cycles, advertising, etc. For example, if you regularly send out bills on a certain day of the month, you'd want to see what the impact is on the days immediately following, and what impact this has on the month as a whole. In these cases it may be necessary to calculate Day Of Month Index Factors. To detect Day Of Month proportions, you compare specific calendar days over a range of months. (See Figure 6 on page 20.) Then you would divide your Day Of Month proportions by the Average Daily Proportions for the month to determine the Day Of Month Index Factors.

Breaking down calling volume to the half-hourly staff planning level is relatively straightforward once you have all the factors available. Also, once you have the factors, it becomes possible to perform intra-week and intra-day forecasts. See Figure 9 below for an example of intra-day forecasting.

The difficult part of call forecasting is estimating the total level of calling volume which will then have to be broken down. This is the subject covered in Part 2 of this series.

Figure 8

Examples of Calculating Day of Week Index Factors For Week With a Holiday
(divide proportion by avg. proportion)

	Prop.	Avg. Prop.	Index Factor
Monday	0	0	0
Tuesday	.345	.25	1.38
Wednesday	.260	.25	1.04
Thursday	.180	.25	0.72
Friday	.215	.25	0.86

Figure 9

Intra-day Forecasting

402	Calls received by 10:30 a.m.
÷ .18	Usual proportion of calls by 10:30 a.m.
2,233	Revised calls forecast for day
x .066	3:30 - 4:00 p.m. proportion
147	Intraday forecast for 3:30 - 4:00 p.m.

Forecasting Calls (Part 2): Forecasting Total Calling Demand

by Gordon Mac Pherson

The difficult part of call forecasting is estimating total call volume. (In Part 1 of this series, we discussed breaking total call volume into its half-hourly components.) Experts teach that there are two primary approaches. One is termed "quantitative" and the other is called "judgmental."

QUANTITATIVE APPROACHES

Quantitative approaches are based purely on quantitative data and statistical analysis, and are theoretically more objective. The major categories within this approach are "time series" and "explanatory."

Time series forecasting uses several statistical techniques, generally based on moving or "rolling" averages. The major time series forecasting methods are: 1) simple or "naive" (rules such as forecast equals last years' same month plus 5 percent); 2) decomposition; 3) simple time series; and 4) advanced time series.

The major explanatory forecasting methods are: 1) simple regression; 2) multiple regression; 3) econometric models; and 4) multivariate methods. (Source: *The Handbook of Forecasting: A Manager's Guide*, edited by Spyros Makridakis and Steven C. Wheelwright, John Wiley & Sons.)

Time series forecasting is popular with vendors of workforce management software. Time series forecasting seeks to project past data patterns or trends into the future. The rationale of unadulterated time series forecasting is that, since there is considerable inertia in most economic and natural phenomena, the current status of many variables is a good predictor of their near-term future status. But, because it is based on inherent assumptions that things will not change and that history will repeat itself, some experts consider it to be "fatalistic." Call center managers' suspicions that they know better than the forecast produced by their ACD management software sometimes leads to overriding such forecasts.

In fact, most time series forecasts are reasonably accurate when the time period covered is three months or less, and time series forecasts have been shown to be consistently more accurate than more subjective methods. Since short-term forecasts are the type least often performed by call centers, and because they offer good accuracy, this could be an area where high gains could be made in planning and staffing.

An example of the results and concept of time series forecasting is shown in Figure 1 (on page 24).

Explanatory forecasting, the other major quantitative approach, attempts to reveal linkage between two or more variables. An example of this technique would be statistically correlating past data on price decreases to the impact on calling volume in order to forecast the impact of a future price decrease.

The complex methods of time series and explanatory techniques go beyond the scope of the present article, and require the use of computers and statistical software packages.

Figure 1

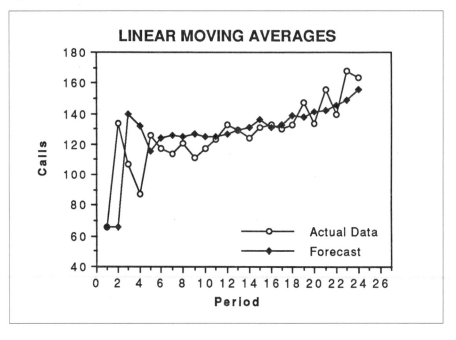

JUDGMENTAL APPROACHES

In contrast to quantitative approaches to forecasting, judgmental approaches go beyond purely statistical techniques, and get into what people think will happen. Judgmental forecasting is the realm of individual intuition, interdepartmental committees, salesforce estimates, executive opinion and market research. Judgmental methods are subjective, and are influenced by politics, personal considerations, over optimism in the sales areas, and other inconsistencies. Nevertheless, judgment is needed and actually present in all forms of forecasting. It is impossible to completely eliminate judgment.

The trick to developing forecasting accuracy is to effectively combine the quantitative and judgmental approaches to forecasting, and recognize the limitations of each. Although uncertainties and inaccuracies in forecasting will never be totally eliminated, they can be minimized by constantly improving technique, and comparing actual to forecasted results.

Part 1 of this series began with the quote: "The future is really the composite of such a multitude of factors that, beyond a certain level, the precise computations of the highly trained and expensively equipped add little over common sense and a more generalized approach to a problem."

Figure 2

How Will Next Year Be Different? - Customer Service

	Jan	Feb	Mar	Apr	May	Jun	Jul	Aug	Sep	Oct	Nov	Dec	Total or Avg
A. Projected Customers	—	—	—	—	—	—	—	—	—	—	—	—	—
B. Calls per Customer	—	—	—	—	—	—	—	—	—	—	—	—	—
C. Base Calls (A x B)	—	—	—	—	—	—	—	—	—	—	—	—	—
D. Activity Level Change				CALLS (+ or -)									
1. New Customers	—	—	—	—	—	—	—	—	—	—	—	—	—
2. Media Attention	—	—	—	—	—	—	—	—	—	—	—	—	—
3. Advertising	—	—	—	—	—	—	—	—	—	—	—	—	—
4. New Rate Structure	—	—	—	—	—	—	—	—	—	—	—	—	—
5. New Terms & Conditions	—	—	—	—	—	—	—	—	—	—	—	—	—
6. New Service Procedures	—	—	—	—	—	—	—	—	—	—	—	—	—
7. New Information Required	—	—	—	—	—	—	—	—	—	—	—	—	—
8. New Product Introduction	—	—	—	—	—	—	—	—	—	—	—	—	—
9. General Activity Level of People Served	—	—	—	—	—	—	—	—	—	—	—	—	—
10. Product Performance	—	—	—	—	—	—	—	—	—	—	—	—	—
11. Competitors Actions	—	—	—	—	—	—	—	—	—	—	—	—	—
12. Other	—	—	—	—	—	—	—	—	—	—	—	—	—
E. Total (add 1 through 12)	—	—	—	—	—	—	—	—	—	—	—	—	—

Figure 2, above, shows how to use common sense and a more generalized approach to forecasting calls in customer service. I learned it from insurance companies.

In a customer service environment, the number of calls is often primarily a function of the total number of customers or constituents in the organization's universe. It's possible to project calls based on historical data showing the relationships between calling volume and total customers (calls per customer) for different months and seasons. Such a forecast should be fairly accurate, assuming that the future repeats the past. The forecast of total customers should be obtained from the marketing department.

Now we add judgment, since the future is unlikely to completely repeat the past. Part D of the form enables you to customize your forecast by adding or deleting calls, based on information you develop from your own and others' input. In all probability, these things are present in the calls per customer figure based on the past, but, if you think the forecast period will produce differences, you need to make logical adjustments.

The list of items in Part D may only partially reflect your own list, which you must create from knowledge of your environment. Please note that the differences you input could be determined through explanatory statistical methods (regression analysis, etc.) or by purely judgmental methods, as listed previously.

FORECASTING SALES CALLS

The topic of sales forecasting is a complex subject unto itself, and will not be covered here. Generally, somebody other than the call center manager does the sales forecast. But the sales forecast and the calls forecast ought to link logically together, otherwise something is wrong somewhere, and somebody had better find out what it is. It will make no sense to "put good business into a bad system." That will happen if advertising and other means of generating prospects succeed, but the call center can't handle the calls properly.

Figure 3 (below) acts as a "sanity check" on whether or not the call center will be able to handle the calls following from a revenue forecast. It requires knowledge of the average sale value in the call center and the conversion factor. Conversion factor is the number of received calls which result in a sale as compared to the total calls received, or the reverse. It can therefore be expressed as a whole number or as a proportion. For example, if it takes four calls on aver-

Figure 3

How Will Next Year Be Different? - Sales

	Jan	Feb	Mar	Apr	May	Jun	Jul	Aug	Sep	Oct	Nov	Dec	Total
A. Projected Revenue	—	—	—	—	—	—	—	—	—	—	—	—	—
B. Average Sale Value	—	—	—	—	—	—	—	—	—	—	—	—	—
C. Number of Sales (A ÷ B)	—	—	—	—	—	—	—	—	—	—	—	—	—
D. Conversion Factor 1 ÷ (orders/calls)	—	—	—	—	—	—	—	—	—	—	—	—	—
E. Projected Calls (C x D)	—	—	—	—	—	—	—	—	—	—	—	—	—

age to make one sale, then multiplying the number of sales expected by four produces an estimate of the number of calls.

Alternatively, you could divide one by four, and then divide the number of sales expected by the result, producing an estimate of the number of calls. The answer will be the same in both cases. (Example: 4.0 x 1,000 = 4,000 or 1,000/.25 = 4,000).

Figure 4 (below) addresses this special case. An example would be a catalog company which mails out advertising that includes a telephone number for responding to the ad. The tricky part here is not shown: Usually, calls coming into a direct marketing call center are the result of overlapping campaigns with different starting and ending times. In any event, the marketing department usually provides the projected orders and their timing, and the call center manager must then make adjustments based on the conversion factor. The complicating factor here is what actually constitutes an order — a single call from a customer, or each item ordered. There's nothing unresolvable about this, though; it just has to be recognized, and the definition agreed to and understood.

CONCLUSION

Forecasting calls is critically important, and you'll never learn all there is to know about it. Remember that the most important step toward greater accuracy is to compare your forecasts to actual results and then ask: Why?

Figure 4

Projecting Calls From A Direct Marketing Campaign

A. Target Audience Size _____

B. Overall Response Rate
(orders/target audience) _____

	Day 1	Day 2	Day 3	Day 4	Day 5	Day 6	Day 7	Day 8	Day 9	Day 10	Day 11	Day 12	Day 13	Day 14
C. Percent Overall Response	—	—	—	—	—	—	—	—	—	—	—	—	—	—
D. Projected Orders (AxBxC)	—	—	—	—	—	—	—	—	—	—	—	—	—	—
E. Conversion Factor 1 ÷ (orders/calls)	—	—	—	—	—	—	—	—	—	—	—	—	—	—
F. Number of Calls (DxE)	—	—	—	—	—	—	—	—	—	—	—	—	—	—

12 Ways to Improve the Predictability of Your Call Center's Workload

by Brad Cleveland

Matching call center resources with the demands of the workload is a critical part of call center planning. This responsibility goes to the heart of Incoming Calls Management Institute's definition of call center management: *The art of having the right number of skilled people and supporting resources in place at the right times to handle an accurately forecasted workload at service level and with quality.*

Accurately predicting the workload presents one of the most important, and often most challenging, steps in this effort. Without a good workload forecast, the rest of call center planning is an uphill battle at best. And when predictions are off the mark, there is a tendency to look to those who do the forecasts for explanations. The people who do the forecasting may be highly trained, equipped with the latest in forecasting software, and armed with every conceivable ACD and database report; but still they will be unable to produce good forecasts if they aren't aware of what marketing is up to or if reps are handling calls inconsistently.

Following are 12 ways to improve the predictability of the workload. Each is outside the realm of what is usually considered to be the forecasting process, yet each is essential to an accurate forecast.

1. Use ACD modes consistently. Each rep has an impact on the components of handling time (talk time and after-call work) and, therefore, on the data that will be used in forecasting and planning for future call loads. When the queue is building, it can be tempting to postpone some after-call work (wrap-up) that should be done at the time of the call. This skews reports, causes planning problems and may lead to increased errors. An important and ongoing training issue is to define ahead of time which types of work should immediately follow calls and which types of work can wait.

When the queue is building, it can be tempting to postpone some after-call work (wrap up) that should be done at the time of the call.

2. Emphasize quality. The pressure of a backed-up queue often forces supervisors and reps to make tough tradeoffs between seemingly competing objectives, such as service level and quality. However, while service level and quality seem to be at odds in the short term, poor quality will negatively impact service level over time by contributing to repeat calls and other forms of waste and rework. This will contribute to workload volatility and inconsistencies. The emphasis should be on handling each call correctly, regardless of how backed up the queue is.

3. Avoid callbacks. Many call centers have discovered the hard way that giving callers the option to leave a message when the queue gets backed up often backfires. For example, a customer may call back only to get perpetual busies, ring-no-answers, voicemail or somebody else in the person's work area ("Sorry, she stepped away for a moment"). And in the meantime, the customer may call again.

A minority of call centers do have successful callback strategies, particularly when reps have to do some amount of preparation in order to handle the calls or when the center is flooded with calls because of a once-in-awhile occurrence. Still, most call centers find that, in the end, it makes more sense to handle the inbound calls when they arrive.

4. Anticipate and manage growth. Analyze the likely impact of growth on your call center. This often takes the form of a chart or document that illustrates the projected costs and time-frames of growing the call center in increments, such as 10 percent growth in call load, 20 percent growth, 30 percent growth and so on. The document should illustrate required lead-times and key decision points associated with things like additional workstations, new or upgraded equipment or a new facility.

5. Develop better ties with other departments. Most of what happens in a call center is caused by something going on outside the operation. The forecast is doomed if strong ties with other departments don't exist. There's no substitute for knowing well in advance when marketing is running the next campaign, when manufacturing is releasing the new products and when finance is redesigning the terms and conditions.

6. Make forecasting a collaborative process. Involve supervisors and lead reps in the forecasting process on a rotating basis. This yields two positive results: 1) they will better understand the pulse of the call load and what's behind the schedules (and they will adhere to them better as a result); and 2) because they are continually dealing with callers, they have their "ear to the ground" and can help to anticipate caller reactions to changes and developments in the marketplace and the organization's services.

7. Track absenteeism. If you are part of a network of call centers or if you have overflow routines established between call center groups, absenteeism in one area has a direct impact on the workload in another. It's important to anticipate absenteeism in advance. And contrary to conventional wisdom, absenteeism is reasonably predictable. For example, in work groups with typical Monday-through-Friday schedules, unscheduled absenteeism tends to be higher on Monday and Friday than on the other days of the week. Have someone track absenteeism and look for patterns.

8. Anticipate the factors affecting caller tolerance. The seven factors of caller tolerance include motivation, availability of substitutes, competition's service level, level of expectations, time available, who's paying for the call and human behavior. Putting some thought into these factors goes a long way toward anticipating caller behavior.

9. Track and manage non-phone activities. Forecasting non-phone activities, such as research and correspondence, is a challenge. Many call center man-

Chapter 2

agers, those who are used to having detailed information on the call load, long for similar reports on non-phone activities. Fortunately, as with inbound calls, these activities often occur in predictable patterns and usually have a strong correlation to other forecasts, such as the inbound call load, units of sales or number of customers (and they are usually a lot less time-sensitive than incoming calls). Investigate the tracking capabilities in your ACD, forecasting/staffing software and computer database. As a last resort, track these activities manually as they occur.

10. Educate callers. The inbound call load tends to be less erratic when callers are aware of other service alternatives (i.e., services via faxback, voice response units or the World Wide Web). Billing inserts, focused advertisements, newsletter articles and customer support sections in user manuals are all examples of ways to better educate callers on the service alternatives available.

11. Minimize transferred and escalated calls. An excessive number of transferred and escalated calls will wreak havoc on the workload forecast. Utilize quality improvement tools, such as flow charts and cause-and-effect diagrams, to address root causes. Common problems include insufficient training, insufficient authority, incomplete or missing database information and poor call-routing design (i.e., calls often end up in the wrong place to begin with).

12. Accomplish as much as possible during talk time. Errors are usually reduced whenever tasks related to inbound calls can be completed with the caller still on the line. Further, the time reps would otherwise spend in more discretionary (and less predictable) work modes, such as after-call work or auxiliary modes, is minimized.

A CALL CENTER-WIDE PROCESS

Call centers with good forecasts do not necessarily have inherently stable environments. Rather, they have established good ties with other departments, pulled in the data required and established a forecasting process they are continually working to improve. They recognize that the responsibility for producing a good workload forecast cannot rest solely on the person or group who "does" the forecasting. Instead, they view forecasting as a call center-wide process and work on all contributing factors.

Understanding the Impact of Non-phone Work

by Ann Smith

In an inbound call center, the agents' primary function is to answer and process incoming calls. There is also, however, a fair amount of "non-phone" work for which agents in most call centers are responsible. But the amount of non-phone work is often severely underestimated or totally ignored in the planning process. There seems to be an assumption that "somehow the work will get done." Failing to include solid calculations of non-phone work in the planning process often results in missed or erratic attainment of objectives.

Successful call centers incorporate non-phone work requirements into resource planning. Combining base staff requirements for calling demand with base staff requirements for non-phone work gives you the total staff (before shrinkage) required to meet both service level and response time objectives. The non-phone workload is calculated hourly, often using the traditional method of "pieces x time" approach. For example, processing five faxes per hour at six minutes each would require a total of 30 minutes, or .5 staff hours for the task. Often, a commitment to respond or complete a non-phone work task is established, and referred to as the response time objective.

Here are prime examples of non-phone work to include in planning:

- Checking/responding to voicemail
- Checking/responding to e-mail
- Reading/responding to paper correspondence
- Receiving/sending faxes
- Attending informal meetings
- Receiving informal training
- Contacting other departments
- Completing follow-up work
- Updating databases

QUANTIFY COMMON TASKS

Even if non-phone work has been calculated and planned for, there is a tendency to overlook the small things that require agents' time. Managers often assume that there is enough time between inbound calls to complete the non-phone work. I recommend that you take a look at your current occupancy rate before making such an assumption. Let's say your occupancy rate is 86 percent (within the "typical" range in our industry); that means each agent will have 14 percent of a half-hour — 4.2 minutes — of free time within the half-hour. Keep in mind that those free minutes are arriving randomly, just like incoming calls. If the calls happen to be evenly spaced, that would mean the 4.2 minutes would be chopped into little 30-second bursts — not much time to get anything done. And even if the 4.2 minutes came in an entire block of time, how much can an agent get done in four minutes?

Here are some suggestions for quantifying common non-phone tasks to enhance planning efforts:
- Ask each agent to list all non-phone activities, including frequency and duration.
- Assign a team to validate actual time required to complete these tasks.
- Check voicemail, e-mail and fax activity reports.
- Peruse ACD system reports for non-ACD calls.
- Assign codes through the ACD to track and identify non-phone activities.
- Study transaction or processing records.
- Conduct "time and motion" studies.

THE DANGERS OF POOR PLANNING

Like the inbound call load, the non-phone workload will vary from day to day, or even half-hour by half-hour. This means it must be forecasted and planned for as it is expected to be performed.

Providing agents with a block of non-phone work time every day without knowing if it is the right amount of time or if it is scheduled at the right time is a dicey practice. There may be times when agents have enough time to complete the tasks, and other times when they don't. Consequently, either the non-phone work will get done at the expense of service level and call quality, or the non-phone work will be sacrificed. In cases where service levels suffer, costs will rise (if your company is paying for the call) and customer satisfaction will drop as callers hang out in the queue. In addition, improperly forecasting and staffing for non-phone work can add up to overtime for agents, again, causing costs to rise.

Failing to forecast and plan for the non-phone work can also lead to burnout and turnover. Agents are often torn between answering new customer calls and keeping promises to other customers. Understaffing and holding agents accountable for incomplete work makes them feel like they are set up for failure.

The call center cannot be appropriately staffed if all work performed is not taken into consideration. You may be managing an incoming call center, but you are responsible for a lot more than just managing incoming calls.

Forecasting Without Numbers

by Henry Dortmans

Forecasting is the most difficult and most important part of call center planning. You must accurately predict the number and length of calls, as well as your calling patterns.

Errors, whether high or low, are expensive. If your estimates are too high, you'll have too many trunks and too many agents waiting idle for calls. If they are too low, the queue will stretch out, busy signals will multiply, agents will burn out and customer service will plummet.

Many companies offer forecasting software that promises to ease the pain and reduce your risk. Just plug in historical data about calling patterns and volumes, add in your assumptions about future trends, and your computer will do the rest. Page after page of charts and graphs will show you exactly how the future will unfold.

That's just fine if your call center has been operational for a while, and if you have been involved long enough to make reasonable assumptions about future changes. But what do you do with a brand new call center: Does the absence of data make accurate forecasting impossible?

In short, the answer is yes. If there is no data at all, then you cannot possibly predict how many trunks and agents you need. Make a wild guess, cross your fingers and get your resume up to date.

But "no data at all" is a rare situation. There is almost always some data available, even if it isn't in the form of neat printouts. It may not be perfect, but some data is better than none. Before you despair, do some detective work.

WHAT CAME BEFORE?

In many cases, new call centers result from taking activities that were previously performed elsewhere and consolidating them into one room, under one management. The task, then, is to get data on those activities.

Take the simplest case — combining two or more automatic call distribution (ACD) systems into one. In most cases, the existing centers will have information about their calling volumes and patterns which can be combined and massaged into a rough picture of what a unified operation might look like.

It's tougher when the new call center is taking over activities that were not well tracked in the past. But it is still possible to get information. Who handled customer service calls previously? How many calls did they receive every day? How long were the calls? You may not get printouts, but you can get anecdotal data by meeting and interviewing people in the departments involved.

If your new center isn't built yet, then those departments are presumably handling the service or sales calls that will come to you. Can your company's Call Detail Recording system be set to track their incoming and outgoing calls for a few weeks? What about the auto-attendant — does it generate statistics on incoming calls to specific departments or extensions? If not, can the people involved keep a manual tally for a week or two? And what about past phone bills? Can you get historical records of toll-free calls?

WHAT'S EXPECTED?

In most cases, if you look hard enough, you can obtain rough numbers. The next challenge is to convert those numbers into estimates of future call activity. Once again, the information that exists may not be in neat printout form.

Call volume forecasts can often be derived from other forecasts. An insurance company that is building its first claims call center may not know how many phone calls it will get, but it certainly has very good data on how many claims it receives each day, month and year, and can project those into the future. Sales forecasts. Product return forecasts. Complaint forecasts. Revenue forecasts. None of these is a perfect substitute for call load forecasts, but they offer a basis for predicting trends. It takes effort and imagination to get those numbers, but they can almost always be found.

> *There is almost always some data available, even if it isn't in the form of neat printouts. It may not be perfect, but some data is better than none.*

REALLY NOTHING?

Occasionally, we do find cases in which there really is no data at all. No history, no forecasts, not even any rough guesses. A new call center is being planned, but no one can say how many calls it will handle, or when.

In such cases, the organization should not be planning a call center yet. Someone, somewhere, has decided that a call center would be a "good thing" without doing any of the basic thinking that such a decision requires. The organization should go back to the basics. What is the center for? What is it expected to achieve? Who will be calling? How often? When? What service level is it expected to deliver?

If no one is willing to ask and answer those questions, then you're back to wild guesses — and you should definitely polish your resume.

Chapter 3:
Understanding Staff Calculations
and Queuing Dynamics

Erlang C, One More Time

by Gordon Mac Pherson

What is Erlang C, and how can you get the Erlang C formula? A little background: Erlang C is the world's classic queuing formula. It was created in 1917 by a Danish telephone company engineer whose last name was Erlang. Basically, it calculates predicted waiting times ("delay") based on: 1) the number of servers, 2) the number of people waiting to be served, and 3) the average amount of time it takes to serve each person.

Of course, if it can do this, it can also predict the resources required to keep waiting times within targeted limits. This is why it can be used by incoming call centers to predict staff required on the phones in order to achieve a specific service level objective, whether expressed as the "average speed of answer" or the percent of received calls which are to be answered within a certain number of seconds.

Erlang C is not the exclusive property of the telecommunications world; it can be used to determine resources required in any situation where people might wait in queue for service — whether that be a ticket counter, a bank of elevators, lanes on a highway or toilets in a sports stadium.

THE ERLANG C FORMULA

For most people, the Erlang C formula is "cute," but not in a usable form. That is why Erlang C also exists in tables. Figure 1, below, shows the formula as it is given in Theodor Frankel's book, *Tables For Traffic Management And Design-Trunking* (ABC TeleTraining Inc., Geneva, IL). Figure 2 (on page 39) shows an excerpt from an Erlang C table in the same book. (Another excellent source for Erlang C tables is *PBX Traffic Analysis - Trunking Tables*, from AT&T.)

As you can see, even using an Erlang C table is not very easy, owing to the fact that you have to take factors from the table (DI and D2) and multiply them against the "holding time" (average talk time plus average after-call work time) in order to get the answers

Figure 1

$$P(>0) = \frac{\dfrac{A_e^{N-A}}{N!} \cdot \dfrac{N}{N-A}}{1 - P + \dfrac{A_e^{N-A}}{N!} \cdot \dfrac{N}{N-A}}$$

where
A = Total traffic offered in erlangs
N = Number of servers in a full availability group
P(>0) = Probability of delay greater than 0
P = Probability of loss — Poisson formula

or by substituting P

$$P(>0) = \frac{\dfrac{A^N}{N!} \cdot \dfrac{N}{N-A}}{\displaystyle\sum_{x=0}^{N-1} \dfrac{A^x}{x!} + \dfrac{A^N}{N!} \cdot \dfrac{N}{N-A}}$$

you need about average delay of all calls and average delay of delayed calls. For example: If D1 in the table in Figure 2 is .295 and holding time is 210 seconds, then .295 x 210 = 62 seconds average delay of all calls. Further, the table is anything but self-evident if you want to relate to the standard service level expression of answering a certain percent of calls received within a certain number of seconds. There is no column or single factor to use for this.

Figure 2

Erlang C Table

A	N	P(0)	D1	D2	P(t) for t =						
---	---	---	---	---	.1	.2	.3	.4	.5	.75	1
22	26	.3163	.079	.250	.212	.142	.095	.064	.043	.016	.006
	27	.2263	.045	.200	.137	.083	.050	.031	.019	.005	.002
	28	.1585	.026	.167	.087	.049	.026	.014	.008	.002	
	29	.1087	.016	.143	.054	.027	.013	.007	.003	.001	
	30	.0729	.009	.125	.033	.015	.007	.003	.001		
	31	.0478	.005	.111	.019	.008	.003	.001	.001		
	32	.0306	.003	.100	.011	.004	.002	.001			
	33	.0192	.002	.091	.006	.002	.001				
	34	.0117	.001	.083	.004	.001					
	35	.0070	.001	.077	.002	.001					
	36	.0041		.071	.001						
	37	.0023		.067	.001						
23	24	.7745	.774	1.00	.701	.634	.574	.519	.470	.366	.285
	25	.5901	.295	.500	.483	.396	.324	.265	.217	.132	.080
	26	.4419	.147	.333	.327	.243	.180	.133	.099	.047	.022
	27	.3249	.081	.250	.218	.146	.098	.066	.044	.016	.006
	28	.2344	.047	.200	.142	.086	.052	.032	.019	.006	.002
	29	.1658	.028	.167	.091	.050	.027	.015	.008	.002	
	30	.1148	.016	.143	.057	.028	.014	.007	.003	.001	
	31	.0779	.010	.125	.035	.016	.007	.003	.001		
	32	.0517	.006	.111	.021	.009	.003	.001	.001		
	33	.0336	.003	.100	.012	.005	.002	.001			
	34	.0213	.002	.091	.007	.002	.001				
	35	.0132	.001	.083	.004	.001					
	36	.0080	.001	.077	.002	.001					
	37	.0048		.071	.001						
	38	.0028		.067	.001						
24	25	.7785	.778	1.00	.704	.637	.577	.522	.472	.368	.286
	26	.5967	.298	.500	.489	.400	.327	.268	.220	.133	.081
	27	.4498	.150	.333	.333	.247	.183	.135	.100	.047	.022
	28	.3331	.083	.250	.223	.150	.100	.067	.045	.017	.006
	29	.2423	.048	.200	.147	.089	.054	.033	.020	.006	.002
	30	.1729	.029	.167	.095	.052	.029	.016	.009	.002	
	31	.1209	.017	.143	.060	.030	.015	.007	.004	.001	
	32	.0829	.010	.125	.037	.017	.008	.003	.002		
	33	.0556	.006	.111	.023	.009	.004	.002	.001		
	34	.0366	.004	.100	.013	.005	.002	.001			
	35	.0325	.002	.091	.008	.003	.001				
	36	.0148	.001	.083	.004	.001					
	37	.0091	.001	.077	.002	.001					
	38	.0055		.071	.001						

Selective Parameters

N = Number of Servers
P(0) = Probability of Delay greater than zero

Table Values

A = Offered Load in Erlang
D1 = Average Delay on all Calls
D2 = Average Delay on Calls Delayed
P(t) = Probability of Delay greater than 1
D1, D2, and t are expressed in multiples of the holding time

Chapter 3

Recognizing this problem, in 1987, I first created a form which enabled me to teach the use of the Theodor Frankel Erlang C tables (Figure 2) in a reasonable amount of time in seminars. This form, shown on page 40 in Figure 3, and will be useful to call center managers who like using tables instead of computer programs.

Far better than either the formula or the tables, is the GW Basic computer language program created by Incoming Calls Management Institute specifically for the use of incoming call center managers. (I wish to express my gratitude to Mr. Lee Goeller who wrote the original program, from which this one is derived in *Business Communications Review*.) The program is in wide use throughout the world. Input and output from the program is shown in Figure 5 (on page 41).

The GW Basic computer language code for the program is shown in Figure 4 (on page 41).* You, or someone on your staff, should easily be able to get this short but powerful program keyed in, modified slightly for your version of Basic if you don't use GW Basic, and saved to disk. Of course, if modification is required from GW Basic, an elementary knowledge of programming in the version of the Basic language you use will be necessary. All things considered, getting the program up and running the first time should take less than one hour.

Figure 3

Erlang C Calculations

Example

(Fill in blanks with appropriate information or calculations.)

To solve for TSRs on the phone:

A. Talk Time _180_ sec.

B. Work time _30_ sec.

C. Service Time (A + B) _210_ sec.

D. Calls per hour _400_

E. Load (C + D) _84,000_ sec.

F. Load in Erlangs (E/3,600) _23.3_

G. Service Level Objective in Seconds _20_ sec.

H. Percent allowed to wait longer than G _20_ %

I. Find Value under "A" in Erlang C table closest to F _23_

J. t = (G/C) = _.095_

K. H/100 _.20_ (converts % to decimal equivalent)

L. Find value for "t" on Erlang C table closest to number on line J _.1_

M. Starting in Erlang C table where value for "A" (line I) & value for t (line L) intersect, find value closest to K _-.218_

N. Find number of TSRs under "N" in Erlang C table on same line as value for line M _27_

In my seminars, I use the sample output shown in Figure 5 to illustrate the dynamic relationships at work in incoming call centers. These relationships (see Figure 6, page 42) make up three Important Immutable Laws of Incoming Call Center Dynamics, and should be carefully studied by anyone who wants to understand the behavior of queues. Please note that Erlang C only tells you the staff you need on the phones, with no allowance for absent staff, lunch, breaks, training, etc.

ERLANG C'S ASSUMPTIONS

In technical terms, Erlang C assumes "infinite sources of traffic" and that "lost calls are delayed." In plain English, Erlang C assumes that all calls are re-

Editor's Note: The Incoming Calls Management Institute now has a computer program called QueueView to do these Erlang B and C calculations for you. For more information visit www.incoming.com

Figure 4

Erlang-C Program for Incoming Call Center Managers

```
10  PRINT "ERLANG C FOR INCOMING CALL CENTERS BY ICMI, INC."
20  INPUT "TALK TIME IN SECONDS=",TA
30  INPUT "AFTER CALL WORK IN SECONDS=",WO
40  INPUT "CALLS PER HALF HOUR=",CPHH
50  INPUT "SERVICE LEVEL OBJECTIVE IN SECONDS=",SLO
60  A=((TA+WO)*CPHH)/1800
70  PRINT "TSRS        P(0)        ASA        DLYDLY        Q1        Q2        SL";
71  PRINT "        OCC        TKLD"
80  N=1: T=1: T1=1: TW=TA+WO
90  IF N<=A THEN 150
100 T2=T*(A/N)*(N/(N-A)): P=T2/(T1+T2): DLYDLY=(1/(N-A))*TW
110 ASA=(P*(1/(N-A)))*TW: Q2=A*(1/(N-A)): Q1=P*Q2: F=SLO/TW
120 SL=1-(P/EXP(F/(1/(N-A)))): TKLD=((TA+ASA)*CPHH)/1800: OCC=A/N
130 PRINT N;
131 PRINT USING "######.#";P*100;
132 PRINT "%";
133 PRINT USING "######.#";ASA;DLYDLY;Q1;Q2;SL*100;
134 PRINT "%";
135 PRINT USING "######";OCC*100;
136 PRINT "%";
137 PRINT USING "######.#";TKLD
140 IF P<.02 THEN 160
150 T=T*A/N: T1=T1+T: N=N+1: GOTO 90
160 STOP
```

Notes: This program is written in GW Basic. Capacity of program is 86 erlangs (hours) worth of traffic (talk + after-call work) — for example, 180 seconds talk, 30 seconds after-call work, 734 calls per half hour.

Figure 5

Sample Inputs and Outputs of Erlang-C Program

Inputs:

Talk Time in Seconds — 180 seconds
After-Call Work Time — 30 seconds
Calls per Half Hour — 250
Service Level Objective — 20 seconds

Outputs:

TSRs	P(0)	ASA	DLYDLY	Q1	Q2	SL	OCC	TKLD
30	82.8%	208.7	252.0	29.0	35.0	23.5%	97%	54.0
31	65.2%	74.7	114.5	10.4	15.9	45.2%	94%	35.4
32	50.7%	37.6	74.1	5.2	10.3	61.3%	91%	30.2
33	38.8%	21.3	54.8	3.0	7.6	73.0%	88%	28.0
34	29.3%	12.7	43.4	1.8	6.0	81.5%	86%	26.8
35	21.8%	7.8	36.0	1.1	5.0	87.5%	83%	26.1
36	15.9%	4.9	30.7	0.7	4.3	91.7%	81%	25.7
37	11.4%	3.1	26.8	0.4	3.7	94.6%	79%	25.4
38	8.1%	1.9	23.8	0.3	3.3	96.5%	77%	25.3
39	5.6%	1.2	21.4	0.2	3.0	97.8%	75%	25.2
40	3.8%	0.7	19.4	0.1	2.7	98.6%	73%	25.1
41	2.6%	0.5	17.7	0.1	2.5	99.2%	71%	25.1
42	1.7%	0.3	16.4	0.0	2.3	99.5%	69%	25.0

Definitions:

TSRs: Number of Telephone Sales or Service Representatives on the phones.
P(0): Probability of a delay greater than 0 seconds. In other words, the probability of not getting an immediate answer.
ASA: Average Speed of Answer. This is the average delay of all calls, including the ones that aren't delayed at all.
DLYDLY: Average Delay of Delayed Calls. This is the average delay only of those calls that are actually delayed.
Q1: Average number of calls in queue at any time, including times when there is no queue.
Q2: Average number of calls in queue when all reps are busy, i.e., when there actually is a queue.
SL: Service Level. The percentage of calls that should be answered in the number of seconds specified, by the number of TSRs (shown in the TSRs column).
OCC: Percent TSR Occupancy. The percentage of the time TSRs will be in either the Talk mode or the After-Call work mode. The balance of the time they are in the Available mode, waiting for the next call.
TKLD: Hours (erlangs) of trunk traffic, which is the product of (Talk Time + Average Speed of Answer) x Number of Calls in an Hour. The answer is converted from seconds to hours, and presented as an hour's worth of load for easy table reference.

Chapter 3

ceived, and that all callers are willing to wait as long as necessary for service.

This is tantamount to saying that you have an infinite number of trunks (incoming telephone lines), that nobody ever gets a busy signal which blocks them from getting in, and that callers have infinite patience for delays once they are in your system. Of course, none of these assumptions are usually true, and both busy signals and lost calls do occur. But, because Erlang C "thinks" the assumptions are true, it has a theoretical tendency to give answers which cause overstaffing. Simply stated, it "thinks" you have

Figure 6

Three Immutable Laws of Service Level Dynamics

Law # 1 — Productivity goes down as service level goes up. It stands to reason that more TSRs can answer a constant number of calls faster than fewer TSRs. So there are the same number of calls, but more TSRs; so the average number of calls handled per TSR goes down.

Law # 2 — Trunk Load goes down as TSRs increase. See Law # 3, which is actually a corollary of this law. The components of Trunk Load are Talk Time and Average Speed Of Answer.

Law # 3 — Average Speed Of Answer goes down as TSRs increase for the same calling load. Self-explanatory.

Figure 7

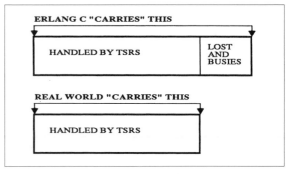

to handle all calls offered, but in reality you only have to handle those which get through to your reps (Figure 7).

As you might have imagined, there is a reasonable defense for the use of Erlang C. First, if you are using Erlang C to help determine staff needed on the phones to meet your carefully considered service level objective, there should theoretically be very little in the way of lost calls or busy signals. Second, if you try to adjust for the calls you estimate will receive busy signals and not call back, or those which abandon and don't call back, you could wind up understaffing if callers, in fact, have a high retrial rate and eventually do get in. Third, other input, such as average talk time, average after-call work time (wrap-up) and number of calls could probably throw your estimate's accuracy off more than this little bit from Erlang C. And fourth, what's wrong with a little overcalculation as a safety factor, if overcalculation really does exist? Most call centers fail to get full effective use of their already authorized headcount due to staff turnover and the time it takes to hire and train replacements.

Today, it is highly debatable whether any truly superior alternatives to Erlang C exist. Erlang C is used internationally by all sorts of telecommunications entities and other experts. In the future, the art of computer simulation will probably replace Erlang C.

The Great Debate:
Erlang C or Computer Simulation?

by Brad Cleveland

Who's going to win the next Super Bowl? Will Netscape or Microsoft win the browser war? What should you use to predict the agents you need, Erlang C or computer simulation? Hey, don't laugh! If you are involved in workforce planning, that's a big question these days.

Ultimately, the debate is centered around how to "get the right people in the right places at the right times." Consequently, the issue impacts service levels, budgeting, costs, agent occupancy and customer satisfaction. Worth looking into, to say the least.

ERLANG C — OLD FAITHFUL

The widely used Erlang C formula (Figure 1) can be used to determine resources in just about any situation where people might wait in queue for service — whether at a ticket counter, in a bank, at an elevator or in a toll booth on an expressway. Erlang C is widely available in the form of free or low-cost PC-based "calculators," and is currently built into virtually all of the full-blown workforce management software packages.

Figure 1

$$P(>0) = \frac{\dfrac{A^N}{N!} \dfrac{N}{N-A}}{\displaystyle\sum_{x=0}^{N-1} \dfrac{A^x}{x!} + \dfrac{A^N}{N!} \dfrac{N}{N-A}}$$

Where

A = total traffic offered in erlangs

N = number of servers in a full availability group

P (>0) = probability of delay greater than 0

P = probability of loss — Poisson formula

Erlang C calculates predicted waiting times (delay) based on three things: the number of servers (i.e., reps); the number of people waiting to be served (i.e., callers); and the average amount of time it takes to serve each person. It can also predict the resources required to keep waiting times within targeted limits — that's why it is useful for incoming call centers.

As with any mathematical formula, Erlang C has built-in assumptions that don't perfectly reflect real-world circumstances. For one, it assumes that "lost calls are delayed." In plain English, that means the formula assumes that calls are queued. No problem with that. The problem is that it assumes callers queue as long as it takes to get an answer or that nobody will abandon. Oops! Erlang C also assumes that you have infinite trunking and system capacity or that nobody will get a busy signal. But some call centers have quite a problem with busy signals. Oops again!

The result is, in a nutshell, Erlang C may overestimate the staff you really need. If some of your callers abandon or get busy signals, your reps won't have

Chapter 3

to handle all of the calls Erlang C is including in its calculations. For a given level of staff, Erlang C predicts that conditions will be worse than they really are. Erlang C also assumes you have the same level of staff on the phones the entire half-hour. In reality, if service level starts taking a nose-dive, you may be able to add reinforcements on short notice.

So, just how bad is Erlang C, anyway? "Erlang C is fairly accurate for good service levels," says Mike Hills, a software developer and recognized expert in traffic engineering. "However, for poor service levels, Erlang C overestimates how bad it really is. Reality will be nowhere as bad as Erlang C predicts."

So why is Erlang C so popular? As you might guess, there are defensible reasons to use it. For one, it's a planning tool, and most call centers are planning to have good service levels. When service level is decent, you should theoretically have little in the way of lost calls or busy signals. If you do have a lot of calls disappearing or getting busy signals, it's probably because you don't have enough staff to handle the load. In that case, who's worried about over staffing? As your staffing more accurately reflects the workload demand, Erlang C will inherently become more accurate.

Figure 2

Advantages of Erlang C	Disadvantages of Erlang C
• Assumes random call arrival and that calls queue if a rep is not immediately available.	• Assumes no abandoned calls or busy signals.
• Is accurate at good service levels, where abandoned calls and busy signals are minimal.	• Assumes "steady state" arrival, or that traffic does not increase or decrease beyond random fluctuation within the time period.
• Is easy and quick to use and available in software form from a wide variety of sources.	• Assumes you have a fixed number of staff handling calls throughout the time period.
• Is the basis for staffing calculations in almost all workforce management software programs.	• Assumes that all agents within a group can handle the calls presented to the group.

Further, if you try to adjust for abandoned calls and busy signals, and retry rates are higher than you estimate, you could end up underestimating staff. (And frankly there's a little industry secret... some call center managers have decided that a little over-calculation as a safety net isn't such a bad thing. They figure that they fail to get full effective use of their already-authorized headcount anyway, due to staff turnover and the time it takes to hire and train replacements.)

Currently, Erlang C is still predominant in workforce management software. It is designed for straightforward environments, like sales calls going here and customer service calls going there. Says Jim Oberhelman of simulator-provider Bard Technologies, "Erlang C was quick, easy and good enough, until ACD and network providers introduced complex routing capabilities."

Oberhelman hits the nail on the head. The realities of today are not as straightforward as they used to be. Elaborate routing contingencies, such as agent groups that overlap, skill-based routing and complex network interflow are common examples. In these applications, Erlang C is "kludge" at best and totally unworkable at worst.

COMPUTER SIMULATION — NEW KID ON THE BLOCK

Enter call-by-call computer simulation. These simulators do for call centers what flight simulators do for pilots or aircraft designers — they enable you to test your staffing and system programming assumptions before you actually implement changes. Consequently, simulation program providers (e.g., Bard Technologies, Systems Modeling Corporation, SIMUL8 and others) are riding a wave. All indications are that there will be increasing demand for these packages.

Figure 3

Advantages of Computer Simulation	Disadvantages of Computer Simulation
• Can be programmed to assume a wide variety of variables, such as overflow, overlapping groups and skill-based routing.	• Takes time to set up and use, and requires a relatively advanced user.
• The assumptions can include lost calls and busy signals.	• Is a stand-alone tool that is generally not integrated with forecasting and staffing modules.
• May be programmed to use the terminology of your ACD vendor, for ready translation into your environment.	• Is generally more expensive than stand-alone Erland C programs.

However, computer simulation also has some down sides. First, simulation is designed for modeling, design and verification, and is generally not meant to be a forecasting and scheduling tool (neither is Erlang C, but Erlang C is often integrated with forecasting and scheduling modules in workforce management systems). It's usually provided as a stand-alone system (although Rockwell's simulator is built into their ACD). "What people have to realize is that simulators provide a way to test ideas about changing your configuration or the way that calls are handled, before introducing the changes," says USAA's Terry Trevino. You will still need your forecasting and scheduling software.

Second, simulation software takes a lot more time to set up and use than Erlang C. Like a flight simulator, you have to run it over and over to identify potential results. That is a phenomenon of its added flexibility, and the time spent will be time saved if you have a complex environment that requires a simulator's perspective. But it takes time to feed variables into the program and interpret the results.

AND THE WINNER IS...

So what should you use? For fairly straightforward environments with good service levels, Erlang C remains an accurate tool. But if you are utilizing complex routing capabilities, we recommend that you use simulation to validate your system configurations and staffing plans. There is something to be said for

Chapter 3

a combination of Erlang C, intuition and experience, but simulation will obviate the need for a lot of guesswork.

In many cases, the ideal solution is a combination of both methodologies. In fact, most of the call centers using simulation today continue to use Erlang C for routine staffing and budgeting. Computer simulation is a much more powerful tool for analyzing specific complex scenarios. But Erlang C remains an excellent, easy-to-use tool for illustrating call center dynamics (i.e., when service level goes up, occupancy goes down) and is predominant in workforce management software.

Whatever methodology you use, remember that no formula or program can perfectly predict the future. As Hills says, "As much as I love it, traffic engineering is only a guide — not omnipotent."

Chapter 3

Skills-based Routing:
The Top Five Problems and Solutions

by Brad Cleveland

Skills-based routing... Intelligent. Flexible. Real-time. The perfect answer to that proverbial call center challenge of getting the right call to the right place at the right time. At least that's the way it's supposed to work.

Available in automatic call distributors (ACDs) for the better part of a decade now, this powerful routing capability is designed to match each caller with the agent who has the skill set best suited to handle the call, on a real-time basis. It's been a boon to the efficiency and quality of services provided by call centers that, by nature, have overlapping groups or complex routing contingencies — and who have managed it well.

But in many cases, skills-based routing, has also created difficult new problems that have tempered or obviated the potential benefits: difficult forecasting challenges, complex staffing puzzles and volatile service levels. As with most new technologies, the benefits of skills-based routing are commensurate with the clarity of the purpose for which it is to serve, and the soundness of the underlying processes by which it is managed.

Enough call centers have used skills-based routing, and for long enough, so that common problems and the lessons they teach have emerged. The top five problems that hamper good results — and the corresponding antidotes — are summarized below. While this order doesn't apply in all cases, it is very typical.

TOP PROBLEM #1: ROSTERED STAFF FACTOR (SHRINK FACTOR) ISSUES

The most problematic issue relates to that question so many call center managers have asked at one time or another as they've wandered the floors: "Where is everybody?" (Rostered staff factor, or shrink factor, numerically represents the percentage of agents not available to handle calls at given times.) Should this be any surprise?

Breaks, lunch, meetings, projects, research, training, other transactions, questions of mode usage... you know the story. There are 101 things that can keep agents from the phones. Because call centers are so timing sensitive, ensuring that people are in the right places working on the right priorities at the right times is a central call center management objective. If planning, communication or priority miscues create problems in normal agent groups, they tend to create havoc in skills-based routing environments. With necessary skills unavailable, calls end up with secondary and tertiary alternatives, sending a ripple effect through the process that can misappropriate available staff and send service level and quality plunging.

Chapter 3

If there are times in the day that service level is volatile for some types of contacts, this issue is a likely culprit. The lesson? There's no substitute for realistically planning and budgeting for the things that keep agents from the phones.

Solution: Spend the time necessary to routinely and realistically anticipate and plan for the activities that keep agents from the phones, by time of day and by skill set.

TOP PROBLEM #2: NOT FORECASTING ACCURATELY AT THE SKILL LEVEL

The queuing formulas and simulation models available for calculating required staff are only as good as the accuracy of input they are analyzing. To anticipate staffing needs, you first need to know how many French-speaking callers you're going to get between 10 a.m. and 10:30 a.m., how the call mix will change throughout the day for the expert group handling call types A, B and C, and when your Mandarin Chinese-speaking agents will go on break. The inability to forecast accurately at the skill level is the Achilles heel of the powerful simulation programs now available.

Good forecasting is often the single, most time-consuming aspect of managing skills-based routing well. But it is worth the investment. The forecast is the foundation on which all resource requirements and budgets are built.

Solution: Invest the time necessary to forecast call load for each mix of calls requiring unique skill sets (e.g., Spanish-speaking calls for service A, Spanish-speaking calls for service B, etc.). Assess the accuracy of forecasted call load vs. actual; if it is routinely off by more than 5 percent to 10 percent by half-hour, consider combining skills to form more manageable groups.

TOP PROBLEM #3: NOT CALCULATING BASE-STAFF REQUIREMENTS ACCURATELY

Purveyors of staffing and workforce management packages are currently engaged in a titanic battle to capture your affections and budget. One of the defining issues is the methodology each uses to calculate staffing requirements in environments with complex routing routines.

The classic queuing formula Erlang C and variations of it are still predominant in workforce management systems. However, since it is designed for straightforward environments where any agent in a group can handle any call, two other alternatives have emerged. One is call center computer simulation, which, like a flight simulator, allows you to test a wide range of variables and assumptions before actually implementing changes. As Bard Technologies, Systems Modeling Corporation, SIMUL8 and other simulation suppliers will attest, demand for this capability is growing briskly. The other alternative consists of various proprietary processes that utilize variations of existing queuing formulas and iterative routines to estimate requirements.

With either alternative, a certain amount of trial and error and a healthy dose of intuition and experience are necessary to accurately model the environment. You will need to play lots of "what if" to get it right.

Solution: Find out what capabilities you currently have for calculating staff. Invest the time necessary to run a wide range of "what if" scenarios to assess your current capacity capabilities and requirements.

TOP PROBLEM #4: POOR ASSUMPTIONS/RATIONALE

In general, skills-based routing works best in environments that require many skills and have many possible combinations of skill sets. Help desks handling a wide variety of complex issues and call centers handling many languages are common examples. Skills-based routing can also help to quickly integrate new agents by initially routing only simple calls or calls of a predefined nature to them.

What skills-based routing can't do is compensate for poor planning, inadequate training or poorly designed information systems. Remember, the core assumption of a call center is pooled groups, where cross-trained agents are equipped to share the workload. All things equal, pooled environments are more efficient than those with specialized groups.

Solution: Keep your eye on the prize, and create an environment that is as pooled as possible. This requires an incessant effort to hire the right people, improve training, improve information systems and reduce staff turnover. In other words, go as far as you can toward obviating the need for skills-based routing.

TOP PROBLEM #5: NO SKILLS-BASED ROUTING MANAGER/COORDINATOR

If all of this sounds time-consuming — it is. Even small call centers have learned through tough, practical experience that it takes what amounts to a full-time person to keep skills-based routing running smoothly. Projecting requirements, assessing current capabilities, updating system programming and adjusting staffing plans and schedules to accommodate evolving circumstances are ongoing activities.

Solution: Create a position for managing skills-based routing. Equip this person or team with the tools, information and authority necessary to predict requirements, make necessary changes to system programming and staffing plans and advise on future requirements.

NO SUBSTITUTE FOR GOOD PLANNING

If there's one lesson that towers above all others, it's this: skills-based routing is no substitute for good planning. To the contrary, good results depend on accurate forecasts, solid staffing calculations, realistic assumptions about staff availability and logical system programming. Skills-based routing is a powerful capability, but it must be managed appropriately to fulfill its promise.

Chapter 3

Calculating Staff Required to Meet E-mail Response Time Objectives

by Brad Cleveland

Effectively managing customer e-mail takes commitment, planning, skilled agents, the right processes and enabling systems. Getting the "right number of skilled people and supporting resources in place at the right times" is at the heart of effective incoming call center management. This article provides a primer on how to accurately calculate the staff required for response time transactions.

THREE TYPES OF 'RESPONSE'

There are three categories of response to a customer e-mail message:

1. Automated reply — this is a system-generated response that automatically sends a reply to customers acknowledging that the e-mail they sent was received and informing them of when to expect a response. This establishes appropriate expectations and minimizes telephone calls or other additional contacts inquiring about the status of the original message.

2. Response — this refers to the response the customer receives when the transaction is actually handled by the call center. The time that elapses between the customer's original message and the call center's response is measured as "response time."

3. Resolution — this is a measure of when the problem or issue is actually resolved. It is used in environments where the call center's initial response may not fully resolve the issue. For example, in a help desk environment, additional research may be necessary; the problem is "resolved" when the matter is handled to completion and the "trouble ticket" is closed.

This discussion focuses on the staff required to meet response time objectives. If additional research or contacts are required for complete resolution, this activity should be reflected in the workload forecast of this group, or another if handled by other agents.

TWO TYPES OF RESPONSE TIME

There are two types of response time: "rolling" and "scheduled" (see Figure 1 on page 51). Rolling response time is hinged on the specific times when each message arrives. For example, if you establish a four-hour response time, a customer who sends a message at 9:03 a.m. should get a response by 1:03 p.m., and one who sends a message at 9:12 a.m. should receive a response by 1:12 p.m.

Scheduled response time, like a dry-cleaning service, is geared around blocks of time. For example, you may commit to handle all messages received up to noon by 5 p.m., and to respond to messages received between noon and 5 p.m. by 10 a.m. the next morning.

Figure 1

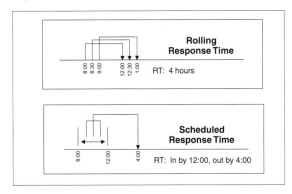

Today, many call centers are establishing straightforward 24-hour scheduled response time objectives, but some in more competitive environments are targeting rolling response times of four and even two hours. In fact, a small but growing number of call centers are handling e-mail messages as they arrive or soon thereafter. If your call center is new to handling customer e-mail, we recommend beginning with a manageable, obtainable objective, such as 24 hours. You can then move toward more aggressive objectives once you are familiar with this aspect of planning and management, and as customer expectations and your business mission dictate.

BASE STAFF REQUIREMENTS

Calculating staff requirements for a workload that does not have to be handled at the time it arrives is generally based on the centuries-old "units of output" approach. Here's the logic: If you get 60 messages that have an average handling time of four minutes, that's four hours of workload. One agent working non-stop could handle the load in four hours. If you need to complete the transactions within two hours, you will need a minimum of two agents working over a period of two hours. So, as with service level and inbound telephone calls, the e-mail workload and response time objective dictate staff requirements. Accordingly, the basic formula for calculating the minimum staff required is:

$$\frac{\text{Volume}}{(\text{RT} \div \text{AHT})} = \text{Agents}$$

Volume is the quantity of transactions you must handle, AHT is the average amount of time it takes agents to handle the transactions (the equivalent of average talk time and average after-call work for inbound telephone calls) and response time is the time you have to respond to customers after receiving their messages. Using the formula, you could handle the 60 messages above in two hours with $60/(120/4) = 2$ agents.

As with any basic formula, there are potential "upgrades" that may better reflect the real-world environment. For example:

$$\frac{\left(\dfrac{\text{Volume}}{(\text{RT - F}) \div \text{AHT}}\right)}{\text{Efficiency}} = \text{Agents}$$

In this variation, F represents the forecast increment, the units of time down to which you forecast the workload (e.g., 30 minutes).

If you include the forecast increment in the calculations as shown, the formula will determine the staff you need from the end of the forecast period to the initial promised response time for those messages. In other words, if you receive the messages between 7:00 and 7:30 and have a four-hour response time objective, the formula will calculate the staff you need from 7:30 to 11:00 (four hours after the messages began arriving). This option adds a conservative component to rolling response time calculations; it ensures that, regardless of when the messages arrive in the course of the half-hour, you will have the staff necessary to handle them within the next 3.5 hours.

Efficiency is a factor that acknowledges that agents cannot handle one transaction after another without any breathing time in-between. We recommend using an efficiency factor of .9 (90 percent) which means agents will have a 10 percent allowance between messages to collect their thoughts and prepare for the next transaction. (You can achieve a similar result by building extra time into AHT before using the basic formula, and leaving efficiency out.)

Figure 2 provides an example of the complete formula. The calculations you make for each forecast increment must be added in layers to arrive at the base staff you need throughout the day. Also, the base staff requirements for any other type of work that your agents handle should be added to these figures.

There are several additional notes to keep in mind:

- The approach outlined here is just one alternative; there are many ways you can slice and dice base staff schedules

Figure 2

Input:
95 messages, 8:00-8:30
Rolling RT, 120 min.
Forecast Incr., 30 min.
Efficiency factor, .9

$$\frac{\left(\dfrac{95}{(120-30) \div 6}\right)}{.9} = 7$$

Therefore, 7 agents required, 8:30 to 10:00

to achieve your objectives. In fact, for the case illustrated in Figure 2, you could have 95 agents rush in and handle all 95 transactions just before the promised response time and still meet your objective. What you are really doing is looking for an efficient way to pour 570 minutes of workload (95 messages x 6 minutes AHT) into your schedules within the promised response time.

- When response time objectives are less than an hour, traffic engineers generally recommend using Erlang C or computer simulation to calculate base staff. This would be a queuing and service level scenario, like inbound telephone calls.
- Breaks, absenteeism and other activities that keep agents from the work need to be added to base staff calculations.

The key point is to get a handle on the e-mail workload and ensure that you are producing sensible staffing and scheduling alternatives. And, as with service level contacts, be sure to periodically glance in the rearview mirror — when all the dust settles, are you accomplishing your objectives as planned?

Chapter 3

Back to the Basics — How Incoming Call Centers Behave (Part 1): The Laws of Call Center Nature

by Brad Cleveland

In any inbound call center, there are predictable, fundamental laws at work. And just as you would need to understand such principles as gravity, lift and velocity in order to design or operate an aircraft, it's imperative to understand the laws that shape how call centers behave in order to manage effectively. This article will introduce key "laws of call center nature" and discuss their importance in planning and management decisions.

OCCUPANCY, SERVICE LEVEL AND GROUP SIZE

Service level is expressed as "X percent of all calls answered in Y seconds." Occupancy is the percent of time during a half-hour that agents who are on the phones are either in talk time or after-call work (wrap-up). The inverse of occupancy is the time agents spend waiting for calls, plugged in and available.

Figure 1, below, and Figure 2 on page 55, which are based on Erlang-C calculations, illustrate the relationship between service level and occupancy: For a given call load, occupancy goes up when service level goes down. In Figure 1, for service level of 80/20, occupancy is 78 percent; if service level drops to 14/20, occupancy goes up to 97 percent. What's the reason for this inverse relationship? If occupancy is high, it's because the agents on the phones are taking call after call after call, with little or no wait between calls. In other words, calls are backed up in queue and service level is low. In the worst scenario, occu-

Figure 1

	SL %			Trunk
Agents	In 20 Sec.	ASA	Occ.	Load
12	14%	561	97%	41.2
13	46%	97	90%	15.4
14	67%	37	83%	12.1
15	80%	17	78%	10.9
16	89%	8	73%	10.5
17	94%	4	69%	10.2
18	97%	2	65%	10.1
19	98%	1	61%	10.1
20	99%	0	58%	10.0

Talk Time: 180 sec; Work Time: 30 sec; Calls: 100

pancy is 100 percent for a long stretch of time because service level is so low that all callers spend at least some time in queue.

The size of the agent group also affects occupancy. At comparable levels of service, a large airline reservation center will have higher occupancy than a small call center serving a regional insurance company. Figure 1 shows that 15 agents are required to handle 100 calls at a service level of 80/20; agent occupancy is at 78 percent. In Figure 2, 40 agents are required to handle a call load three times as large and at the same service level, with occupancy at 88 percent.

Figure 2

Talk Time: 180 sec; Work Time: 30 sec; Calls: 300				
Agents	SL % In 20 Sec.	ASA	Occ.	Trunk Load
36	26%	171	97%	58.4
37	46%	68	95%	41.4
38	61%	36	92%	36.0
39	72%	21	90%	33.6
40	81%	13	88%	32.2
41	86%	8	85%	31.4
42	91%	5	83%	30.9
43	94%	4	81%	30.6
44	96%	2	80%	30.4
45	97%	1	78%	30.2
46	98%	1	76%	30.2

Chapter 3

Occupancy cannot be directly controlled. That can be a tough case to make in the budgeting process. The reality, though, is that the time agents spend waiting for calls — nine seconds here, 18 seconds there, two seconds there — is a necessary part of a good service level and is driven by how calls are arriving. Sure, even with very good forecasts and schedules, there will be times when you either have too many or too few agents; it only makes sense for them to do other activities when there is time to do so. But don't expect them to get other work done and still meet your service level objective if, according to Erlang C or computer simulation, you have no more than the minimum staff required to handle the call load.

At the individual level, standards on number of calls handled are usually inherently unworkable or unfair. Agents can't control occupancy, and those assigned to larger groups, busier shifts or shifts that have lower service levels, will naturally have the opportunity to handle more calls. On the other hand, agents should be responsible for their "adherence factor," or how well they adhere to their schedules. The terms occupancy and adherence factor are often incorrectly used interchangeably. But they have very different meanings and actually have an inverse relationship — when adherence to schedule improves (goes up), service level will get better and occupancy will drop.

As anyone who has handled calls knows, extended periods of high occupancy are stressful. Studies generally conclude that agents begin to burn out when occupancy is higher than around 90 percent to 92 percent. Unfortunately, occupancy tends to feed on itself. When it's high to begin with, agents need and will often increasingly take breaks from the action. They may sign off or, more subtly, stretch out talk time and/or after-call work time, which will cause service level to drop and occupancy to go higher still. (If you are running into this problem, read on).

THE LAW OF DIMINISHING RETURNS

The law of diminishing returns says, "When successive individual telephone agents are assigned to a given call load, marginal improvements in service level that can be attributed to each additional agent will eventually decline." For example, Figure 2 shows that 36 agents will provide a service level of 26 percent answer in 20 seconds with an ASA (average speed of answer) of 171 seconds. With just one more agent, service level jumps to 46/20 and ASA drops to 68 seconds — a quantum improvement. Adding one more person yields another big improvement. But keep adding staff, and the returns begin to diminish. At some point, the cost of adding additional staff outweighs the small improvements in service that they would bring.

Call centers that struggle with a low service level ought to like this law — it often doesn't take a lot of resources to improve things dramatically. On the other hand, those who want to be the "best of the best" in terms of service level find it takes a real commitment in staffing. That is why many call centers have a target service levels such as 80/20 or 90/20 versus 100/20 or 100/0.

If you find yourself short-staffed, you'll notice that delay grows exponentially and occupancy quickly becomes high. Here are three proven strategies for avoiding these problems:

- Ensure that your staffing calculations are as accurate as possible. If service level is volatile throughout the day and week, or frequently below your objective, the fix may go to the fundamentals of managing a call center — a good forecast and schedules that better match staff to the workload.
- Make every agent aware of how much they contribute, even if they are tempted to feel like just "one of many." Explain service level and show them the call load patterns so they know how important schedule adherence is.
- Provide real-time queue information to supervisors and agents so they can adjust their activities according to real-time conditions.

Part 2 of this series (on page 57) will pick up with these and other immutable laws and further discuss their implications on planning and management.

Back to the Basics — How Incoming Call Centers Behave (Part 2): The Powerful Pooling Principle

by Brad Cleveland

There are predictable, fundamental laws at work in an incoming center. In order to manage effectively, it's imperative to understand how these laws shape how call centers behave. Part 1 of this series discussed the relationship between service level and agent occupancy, and the impact of staffing levels on service level and agent occupancy. In Part 2, we'll look at how staffing levels impact the load on the trunks (and, therefore, network costs), and discuss the management decisions surrounding the "powerful pooling principle."

AGENTS IMPACT TRUNK LOAD

When more telephone agents are assigned to handle a given call load, the load that the trunks (telephone lines) must handle goes down. The converse is also true: When fewer agents are available to handle a given call load, trunk load goes up because delay increases (Figure 1). Consider checking in for a flight — fewer agents at the counter means longer lines. In a call center, each person waiting in queue requires a trunk. You can see this relationship in the last column of the table in Figure 2 (on page 58), which gives the load to be carried by the trunks, expressed in erlangs (hours) — (talk time + average speed of answer) X number of calls in an hour (calculations are based on Erlang C). To determine ACD system capacity required, the following inputs are necessary:

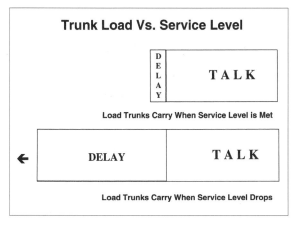

Figure 1

- Calling load, which includes the number of calls the ACD will be required to handle at peak capacity, average talk time and average after-call wrap-up. Note: Since wrap-up does not show up on trunking reports, trunk reports alone are insufficient to predict ACD capacity requirements.
- Service level objective, or "X percent of calls to be answered in Y seconds."
- Agent scheduling factors that accommodate absenteeism, lunch, breaks, training and other realities which will keep agents from the phones.

Call center managers should know these numbers — often factors of 1.2 to 1.5 (for example, if Monday's 9 a.m. factor is 1.3 and 20 agents need to be "plugged in," 26 agents will need to be scheduled, or 20 X 1.3).

Once the above inputs are used to calculate staff, trunks can be configured to carry the load (plus any VRU load not reflected in delay, etc.). Since delay is a function of staffing, staffing must be calculated before trunking. Further, the costs on the network are directly related to staffing levels. The major message from this immutable law is that staffing, system, and network resources must be planned and calculated in sync because they are inextricably associated.

THE POWERFUL POOLING PRINCIPLE

The pooling principle is a mathematical fact, based on the laws of probability. It states: Any movement in the direction of consolidation of resources will result in improved traffic-carrying efficiency. Conversely, any movement away from consolidation of resources will result in reduced traffic-carrying efficiency. Note the efficiencies illustrated in Figure 3 (on page 59); for example, one combined group of 15 agents can handle the same call load at the same service level as two groups of nine agents.

To the degree you can combine smaller groups of agents into larger groups without increasing average handling time, you can: a) handle more calls at the same service level with the same number of agents; b) handle the same number of calls at the same service level with fewer agents; or c) handle the same number of calls at a better service level with the same number of agents.

The pooling principle is a consideration at the highest levels of strategic planning (i.e., call center consolidation

Figure 2

Talk Time: 180 sec; Work Time: 30 sec; Calls: 300				
	SL %			Trunk
Agents	In 20 Sec.	ASA	Occ.	Load
36	26%	171	97%	58.4
37	46%	68	95%	41.4
38	61%	36	92%	36.0
39	72%	21	90%	33.6
40	81%	13	88%	32.2
41	86%	8	85%	31.4
42	91%	5	83%	30.9
43	94%	4	81%	30.6
44	96%	2	80%	30.4
45	97%	1	78%	30.2
46	98%	1	76%	30.2

or networking multiple sites) down to more specific decisions about how far to proceed with cross-training. In one sense, pooling resources is at the heart of what ACDs do. In fact, when ACDs first came into the market in the early 1970s, the big challenge was to get users to abandon the "clientele" approach, or the need to reach specific individuals. Further, geography no longer matters. In some cases, agents can work out of their homes if the proper telecommuting environment is established. And, networked ACDs are virtually a "must-do" for organizations with multiple call centers.

Intelligent call processing capabilities in modern ACDs provide the means to bring diverse resources and skills together at just the right time. For example, skills-based routing enables the skills of each agent (i.e., knowledge of products or services or languages spoken) to be defined and identified to the ACD. Then, specific types of incoming calls can be matched with specific skills — assuming a good planning and management process is in place so the right agents are, in fact, available at the right times.

Figure 3

Calls	SL	Agents Req.	Occ.
25	80% in 20 sec.	5	58%
50	80% in 20 sec.	9	65%
100	80% in 20 sec.	15	78%
500	80% in 20 sec.	65	90%

*Assumption: Calls last 3.5 minutes.

But it's important to remember that the most efficient environment would be one where any call could be handled by any agent. Further, if capabilities such as skills-based routing are implemented poorly, the number of contingencies can multiply beyond the call center's ability to manage them, reducing efficiencies and causing poor service. One thing is certain — as real and pervasive as the pooling principle is, it is not an all-or-nothing proposition. There is a continuum between pooling and specialization. Call centers should specialize when it clearly is necessary (i.e., for different languages or significantly different product lines), but they should also look for cross-training opportunities wherever practical.

IN A NUTSHELL

This article series summarized important immutable laws:
• When service level goes up, occupancy goes down (at a given call load).
• With more staff delay goes down and, therefore, trunk load goes down (at a given call load).
• The law of "diminishing returns."
• The "powerful pooling principle."
• Larger groups have higher occupancy (at a given service level).

These immutable laws shape the way call centers behave, and understanding them is a prerequisite to understanding the call center environment and managing it effectively.

Chapter 3

Chapter 4:
Determining Schedule
and FTE Requirements

Getting People in the Right Place at the Right Times (Part 1):
Rostered Staff Factor

Getting People in the Right Place at the Right Times (Part 2):
Work Types vs. Scheduling Requirements

Staffing Strategies: Matching Supply and Demand

Calculating FTEs (Part 1):
Why Staff Shrinkage Perplexes Your CFO — and Shrinks your Budget

Calculating FTEs (Part 2):
The Science and Judgment Behind FTE Budgets

Getting People in the Right Place at the Right Times (Part 1): Rostered Staff Factor

by Brad Cleveland

Have you ever looked at a supervisor monitor or counted your reps on the floor and wondered, "Where in the world is everybody?" If so, you're not alone. I don't know of a call center manager who hasn't asked that question at one time or another.

Where are they? On break? In the restroom? Maybe they ran out of something they need or are in training. Maybe they are doing non-phone work, getting help from someone or helping somebody else. Or maybe they went home sick. The list could go on and on. The reality is, you can do a good forecast of exactly how many people you need on the phones, and still miss your service level objective by a long shot because you don't have the staff you expected on the phones.

In some respects, this issue is becoming even more challenging (or at least more critical) than ever before. For example, a growing number of organizations are serving customers through online services. This traffic is growing by leaps and bounds and, in most cases, is being handled by a small but proliferating number of call center staff. And although this activity is less time-sensitive than randomly arriving incoming calls, it is a type of non-phone work that must be planned for. Further, the trend toward skills-based routing and other forms of custom call-handling which require specific skills means that service level will deteriorate more quickly if reps aren't plugged in when expected.

An important part of the solution is to accurately calculate rostered staff factor (RSF). RSF, alternatively called "shrink factor" or an "overlay," is a numerical factor that leads to the minimum staff needed on schedule over and above the staff required on the phones to achieve a targeted level of service. It is calculated after base staffing requirements are determined and before schedules are organized (see Figure 1).

Figure 1

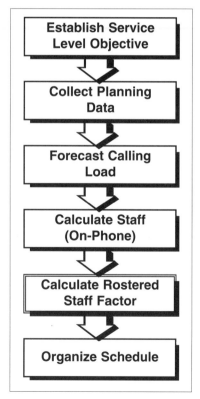

Establish Service Level Objective

Collect Planning Data

Forecast Calling Load

Calculate Staff (On-Phone)

Calculate Rostered Staff Factor

Organize Schedule

Chapter 4

Figure 2 (below) illustrates the simple mechanics necessary to calculate rostered staff factor. Staff required on the phones from previous planning steps are entered into the first column. The next three columns reflect absenteeism, breaks and training as they now occur. (Note: You may want to break these columns down further. For example, absenteeism can be divided into planned absenteeism, such as vacations, and unplanned absenteeism, such as sick leave). The "On Schedule" column is the sum of all previous columns. Finally, the "Rostered Staff Factor" column is the result of dividing staff required on schedule by staff required on the phones.

The result is a set of RSFs that you then multiply against the number of people you will need on the phones when assembling future schedules. For example, if you are putting together a schedule that begins several weeks from now, and you need 32 people on the phones between 8 a.m. and 8:30 a.m., you will need to schedule 40 reps (32 x 1.25) for that half-hour, plus any staff required to be in special training or to do non-phone work or anything else not included in the RSF calculation.

Why bother with RSF if you know how many reps you will need by adding the columns together? Because, you are coming up with a table of factors that will prevent you from having to add these columns together in the future, as base staffing requirements change. RSF not only improves accuracy, it is a big time saver.

RSF should be calculated for each half-hour (or for added accuracy, each 15-minute increment), for each day of the week. However, some call center managers use an ongoing, fixed percentage for RSF (such as 15 percent or 20 percent). That will not be acceptably accurate because the things that keep staff off the phones fluctuate throughout the day and week. For example, absenteeism is usually higher on Mondays and Fridays. And the number of staff on breaks will vary throughout the day.

The major assumption behind rostered staff factor is that the proportion of staff off the phones for reasons accounted for by RSF will stay constant in the future, relative to onphone staff requirements. In other words, if one person is on break in a group of 10, 10 people will be on break in a group of 100.

Figure 2

Rostered Staff Factor Calculations

	Agents on Phone From Erlang C	Absent	Break	Training	On Schedule	Rostered Staff Factor
08:00-08:30	28	3	0	4	35	1.25
08:30-09:00	30	3	0	4	37	1.23
09:00-09:30	37	3	4	4	48	1.30
...						
...						

$$\text{Rostered Staff Factor} = \frac{\text{On Schedule}}{\text{On Phone}}$$

While breaks and absenteeism should almost always be included in RSF calculations, other activities often require a measure of good judgment. For example, Figure 2 shows training included in RSF. Should it be? Clearly, if training schedules frequently change and/or require differing proportions of staff, keep it out of RSF and instead factor it into schedules on a case-by-case basis. But if it happens in predictable proportion to the staff required on the phones, include it.

The same holds true for any type of non-phone work. If it happens in proportion to the base staff required (i.e., correspondence or outbound calls that are associated with, but do not have to immediately follow, inbound calls), it can feasibly be included in RSF. If not, it should be scheduled independently of RSF (in either case, remember that after-call wrap-up is already accounted for in base staffing requirements). Assess it against the core assumption, which is that it will happen in proportion to the on-phone staff requirements.

In many incoming call centers, RSF ranges between 1.1 and 1.4 throughout the day, meaning that a minimum of 10 percent to 40 percent additional staff are required on schedule over those required on the phones. If non-phone activity is included in RSF, and there is a lot of it, RSF can be as high as 2.0 (common in small, specialized help desks with extensive off-line research). Like any planning, go back and check how accurate the RSF calculations were compared to actual results and adjust accordingly. Further, you will have to adjust RSF over time for things like vacation season and major changes in training schedules.

An added advantage of calculating RSF is that it will force you to assess these activities. Should they be happening when and to the degree that they are? Some changes may provide better coverage or make scheduling easier or more acceptable.

Chapter 4

Getting People in the Right Place at the Right Times (Part 2): Work Types vs. Scheduling Requirements

by Brad Cleveland

Call centers of yesteryear were, by most accounts, simpler to schedule for than their modern-day descendants. A number of trends have contributed to the complexity. For example, many call centers support a broader range of products and services than they did in the past. Further, technology has enabled many simple transactions to be automated, leaving reps with more varied and demanding calls, which often necessitate more off-line research, follow-up and training. And customers are utilizing a variety of communications media other than the telephone to interact with organizations (i.e., e-mail, voice processing, the Internet and fax). In short, most call centers are doing much more than just "answering the phones."

Nonetheless, the core objective of staffing and scheduling remains the same: Get the right number of properly skilled and equipped reps in place at the right times to handle the forecasted call load at service level and with quality. This involves accurately calculating base staff requirements (on-phone requirements) and Rostered Staff Factor (RSF). It also requires effectively planning and managing the growing variety of other events and activities that tug on reps' time. As illustrated below, how an activity is categorized will dictate how it is accommodated in staffing and scheduling requirements. Understanding this framework should make this part of planning more accurate and manageable.

IDENTIFY PHONE AND NON-PHONE ACTIVITIES AND EVENTS

An important prerequisite to effective staffing and scheduling is to identify the various activities and events that will occupy reps' time. Examples include:

- Handling ccontacts
- Attending meetings
- Doing research (list by major type)
- Doing special projects (list by major type)
- Going to the bathroom
- Doing administrative work
- Handling correspondence
- Getting supplies
- Getting assistance
- Providing assistance
- Going on break/lunch
- Being called away by the personnel or other department
- Attending training

Chapter 4

- Receiving a performance appraisal
- Providing a performance appraisal
- Absent (planned/unplanned)

Take some time to make a list that is as specific to your environment as possible (you do not need to measure the time each activity requires or takes at this stage).

CATEGORIZE EACH ACTIVITY

Next, classify each of the items on the list according to the following four major categories. How you categorize each activity or event determines how it is factored into staffing and scheduling requirements.

1. Work that is part of the incoming call load. This includes anything that should be a part of talk time or after-call work (wrap-up). Talk time includes everything from "hello" to "good-bye." After-call work is the activity that should immediately follow inbound calls. If the queue is building, it can be tempting to postpone after-call work, but that will skew reports, cause planning problems and may lead to increased errors. Also, take note of any activities that are currently a part of talk time or after-call work but should not be, such as unrelated correspondence or breaks.

Determining Staffing/Scheduling Requirements: The activities that are a part of talk time and wrap-up make up the randomly arriving incoming call load, which determines base staffing requirements. Because the work arrives randomly, staff must be calculated using either a queuing formula that takes random arrival into account (i.e., Erlang C) or a computer simulation program that can realistically simulate random call arrival. Base staffing requirements should be calculated for each rep group (split, queue) or each combination of defined skill sets down to half-hour or 15-minute increments.

2. Activities that are related to RSF. Rostered Staff Factor is a numerical factor that leads to the minimum staff required on schedule over and above the staff required on the phones to achieve a targeted level of service. It is calculated after base staffing requirements are determined and before schedules are organized, and includes activities that occur in proportion to the base staff requirements, such as breaks, absenteeism and training.

Determining Staffing/Scheduling Requirements: Activities proportionally related to base staffing requirements should be part of RSF calculations (i.e., breaks, training and absenteeism). RSF is calculated for each rep group or each combination of defined skill sets down to half-hour or 15-minute increments.

3. Measurable activities that are not a part of base staffing or RSF calculations. This category may sound a bit vague, but, in practice, the activities that it includes are usually apparent. Examples include meetings, correspondence, research (that which is not a part of talk time or after-call work) and outbound calling (that which is not a part of talk time or after-call work). These activities are generally scheduled to occur as the inbound load permits or as the priority of the activity dictates.

Some call center managers have observed that, at any given time, between 3 and 4 percent of staff may be tied up in "unproductive" activity.

To accurately schedule these items, they must be reasonably measurable and predictable. That's easy enough with something like a meeting. (Sure, holding a meeting without destroying service level can be quite a challenge, but scheduling a meeting is straightforward.) However, measuring and forecasting activities such as research and correspondence can be more of a challenge. And many call center managers, used to having detailed information on the call load, long for similar reports on these types of non-phone work. Fortunately, as with inbound calls, these activities often occur in predictable patterns and usually have a strong correlation to other forecasts, such as the inbound call-load, units of sales or number of customers.

Some of the alternative methods of measuring these activities include:

- Using an ACD feature often called "sign out with reason," whereby reps enter a code into the system as they sign out which is identified with the activity they are about to do. The ACD can then generate reports on how long each rep or group spends on each defined activity.
- Using scheduling software that allows for non-phone activity tracking.
- Using database software packages that can provide activity reports. For example, transactions received and sent via computer online services or the Internet can be readily tracked.
- Tracking outbound calls, which are often a part of this category, using the ACD.
- Having reps manually log non-phone activities.

Determining Staffing/Scheduling Requirements: Since these activities are not as time-sensitive as randomly arriving calls, staff is calculated by the conventional method of dividing units of projected work by an average productivity figure (i.e., if there are 50 letters to which to respond, and an average rep can process 10 in an hour, the equivalent of five staff-hours are required). Staffing requirements for these activities are then added as a second tier to base staffing and RSF calculations. These activities are often scheduled into periods when the call load is relatively light.

4. "Unproductive" time. This category includes the many miscellaneous activities that can't or shouldn't be tracked and which don't fit into any of the above categories. Examples include going to the bathroom, getting supplies and momentarily getting called into another area. Some call center managers have observed that, at any given time, between 3 percent and 4 percent of staff may be tied up in "unproductive" activity. While this degree of precision is not feasible or necessary in smaller groups (say, 20 or fewer reps), it is often a necessary margin in groups of 100 or more.

Chapter 4

Determining Staffing/Scheduling Requirements: Some call center managers schedule 3 percent or 4 percent extra staff over base staffing requirements.

ESTABLISH REAL-TIME PRIORITIES

Not everything can be perfectly predicted and scheduled, so there has to be some give and take. An important part of planning is to clarify, ahead of time, as feasible, what the priorities are as circumstances change.

One final point: Staffing and scheduling, like anything, take practice. You'll learn a ton by taking the time to carefully compare what actually happens to what was scheduled to happen.

My hope for this article is that it helps you understand how different types of activities are factored into staffing/scheduling requirements, and provides a framework for assessing how new activities will fit in.

Chapter 4

Staffing Strategies: Matching Supply and Demand

by Brad Cleveland

Call traffic tends to fluctuate significantly throughout the day, month and year. How can you ensure that your center is staffed with an adequate number of agents in place, without being overstaffed?

There are quite a few alternatives that may exist, depending on your situation. This article lists (with a comment or two) some of the strategies call centers are using. Obviously, not all will be available to every call center, and each strategy requires its own setup and planning. The purpose here is simply to identify choices.

Naturally, a prerequisite to "matching supply and demand" is to predict, with some degree of accuracy, the number of people you need on the phones throughout the day, week, month and year. This means accurately forecasting the calling load for each answer group, and knowing how to use the forecast to determine the number of staff needed.

The following list is not in any particular order. Check the strategies you are not using to see if they might be feasible in your situation:

1. Adjust breaks, lunches, meetings and training schedules. It's a bit disheartening to do a superb job of forecasting and planning, only to see the everyday things that keep agents away from the phones come between you and your service level objective. Many look for the easy fix here. They simply add something like 25 percent to the average number of agents they need in a day. This doesn't work — it can't! There is no substitute for scheduling these things in advance, and assessing their impact on how many agents will be available for the phones, down to at least the half-hour. Many go even further and plan in 15-minute increments, because these things tend to happen in 15-minute blocks of time (for example, breaks are usually 15 minutes long, lunch may be 45 minutes, and training may be 1 hour and 15 minutes).

2. Plan around absenteeism. Absenteeism is usually quite predictable (unless the flu sweeps through!). It's almost always higher on Monday than on Wednesday, and will be higher during vacation season. Make the effort to forecast and plan around absenteeism well in advance.

3. Stagger shifts. For example, start one shift at 8 a.m., one at 8:30 and so forth, until the center is fully staffed around the day's traffic peak, whatever time that may be. Be sure to "tweak" these shifts as necessary — calling patterns can subtly move out from under what were once good schedules.

4. Use part-timers. Some call centers cannot use part-time help because of union agreements or logistics (complex call center services requiring extensive training). If available and practical, this is a popular strategy.

5. Use "internal" part-timers. This approach is sometimes called the "Reinforcement Method." When phone-answering duties are combined with non-phone types of tasks, such as computer correspondence, outbound calling or data-entry, agents assigned to these collateral duties can act as reinforcements when the calling load gets heavy. This is similar to being able to bring in part-timers on an hourly, half-hourly or even five-minute basis.

6. Create a "swat team." This takes the reinforcement method one step further. Excerpts from a *Wall Street Journal* article (July 16, 1990) describe how one mutual fund "keeps its investors happy: The phone calls are pouring in so fast that what Vanguard calls its Swiss Army has been mobilized to answer them. This army consists of reservists: employees such as Curtis Hilliard, a Vanguard lawyer... Sometimes things get so busy, Mr Hilliard says, that 'you see the chairman down here answering the phone.'"

Granted, this may be impractical for many. But are your calls important enough to warrant at least some additional help from some people elsewhere in the organization? Setup is not trivial. Plan on tackling training, scheduling, pay and cultural issues.

7. Forecast and plan for regular non-phone work. If you can accurately forecast incoming call loads (and you can), then you can forecast non-phone work. This is an added measure of flexibility. Good planning will ensure that a full staff is on the phones during peak times. Even if your agents are already swamped 100 percent of the time, manage this area well. After all, there are degrees to how bad things can get!

8. Offer overtime. No additional training necessary here, and many agents will volunteer for the extra work. The obvious consideration is whether they can effectively handle it. There are good reasons for the legal limits to the amount of continuous hours pilots and truck drivers can work.

9. Give agents the option of leave without pay (LWOP). This is a popular strategy on slower days, and there are usually enough agents willing to take you up on it.

10. Offer split shifts. For most, this strategy is not practical, but I've seen it work handsomely in some situations. If you hire college students, for example, they may prefer to work in the morning and evening, leaving themselves free to attend classes during the day.

11. Create flexible shifts. We humans are a diverse lot. Given the choice, some of us would prefer to work fewer days, with more hours per day, while others would prefer to work fewer hours in a day, even if that means a six- or seven-day work week. Giving your agents these types of choices means additional flexibility for you. This is routine in call centers with extended hours.

12. Arrange for some agents to be "on call." Again, this strategy is impractical for many, but can work well for call centers who must react to events that cannot be precisely predicted (e.g., utilities during storms, or cataloguers during the initial days of a new mail drop).

13. Use hiring to your advantage. One criterion of a "qualified" job applicant could be the hours they can (and can't) work.

14. Make slack time count. If overstaffed, make the slack time count. This can include upselling, cross-selling, working on special projects, training, etc. The point is to think through the priorities on an ongoing basis, before the fact.

15. Reassign agents from one answer group to another. Every answer group will have a unique calling pattern. Crosstrain the more experienced agents from one or more groups, and reassign them as necessary.

16. Overflow calls. Overflow is popular, whether to another answer group, another call center or to an outside source such as a service bureau. As with reassigning agents or using internal part-timers, there are planning, scheduling and training issues involved.

17. Set up specialized staff to handle tough calls. Difficult calls can really slow things down. Agents have to fumble for information and/or get help from others who may or may not be available. Some call centers prepare by setting aside a small group of their best agents to be available for the toughest calls.

18. Utilize supervisors wisely. When volumes are pouring in, what makes more sense: Putting your supervisors and managers on the phone or making sure they are available to answer questions and direct traffic? Ask them. There's no universal approach here.

19. Utilize simple system announcements. Tell callers when the best times to call are, announce extended hours and tell them about other service alternatives (such as using fax or an automated system). Simple announcements can offload a lot of routine calls. For example, utilities can announce that: "If you are calling about a power outage in the Lakeview neighborhood, we have identified the problem and expect power to be restored by 3 p.m. If you require further assistance, please stay on the line..."

20. Take messages for later callback. This seems to be a trend, and it can work if callers are willing. However, consider well the new problems created. How do you ensure that you return the outbound calls? What do you do when you get junior on the phone who says that Mom or Dad is gone? What about voicemail? In many cases, it makes more sense to staff up for the original inbound calls.

21. Prioritize calls. If you can't handle every call in short order, give priority to the most important customers. They can be identified by the number they dial, information they enter into the voice processing system or the number they are calling from.

22. Telecommute. Sending calls to agents who are at home or in satellite offices is a trend that is taking awhile to catch on, but promises to catch on. Plan for it!

23. Prioritize agent time. Whether by blinking lights on phone sets or real-time queue status displays on reader boards, agents need to know when they should hold off on break room visits for a few minutes. Of course, if Service Level is chronically bad, this approach won't work. If anything, it will just increase stress. They'll go to the breakroom anyway, and stay longer!

24. Sacrifice service level for a planned period of time. It may be unrealistic for some customer service centers to meet service level during the initial weeks of a new product introduction. Some choose to "sacrifice" Service Level for three to six weeks and rely on customers to understand. This must be carefully planned and controlled.

Chapter 4

25. Busy out some of your trunking capacity. This one is enticing, because it drives costs down (in the short term) and service level up (for the lucky callers who get through). Don't be overly enamored or dependent, though. Nobody likes to encounter a busy.

26. Work at the source. This is an activity of forecasting, but I include it here because it is so important. Develop strong and ongoing ties with others in the organization. Know when marketing is running the next campaign, when manufacturing is releasing the new products, when finance is redesigning the terms and conditions. Many use billing inserts, advertisements and the like to educate callers on the best times to call, the information to have ready, etc.

If you can accurately forecast incoming call loads (and you can), then you can forecast non-phone work.

Other alternatives which merit more discussion than space allows include automation that can handle a portion of the calls (such as a voice processing system) or shorten calls (such as with better online information), training (which should always be a top priority) and establishing productivity incentives. Don't lose sight of the fact that you need a certain minimum number of people to handle your workload, no matter how savvy your use of any of the above strategies.

Chapter 4

Calculating FTEs (Part 1):
Why Staff Shrinkage Perplexes your CFO
— and Shrinks your Budget

by Brad Cleveland

If you're like most other call center managers on the planet, there's been a day or two when you've drifted across the floor, watching service level plummet, and wondered aloud, "Where is everybody?" It's not a comfortable feeling.

It's even less comfortable to be inadequately prepared to answer when your Chief Financial Officer (CFO) asks YOU some variation of the above question: "Where are they, anyway? Just how are you call center folks spending your time?"

Getting "the right number of properly skilled people and supporting resources in place at the right times to handle an accurately forecasted workload at service level and with quality" is at the heart of effective call center management. Accomplishing this objective requires accurate analysis and management at many levels, from long-term planning to intraday staffing adjustments.

But the foundation upon which your call center capacity is built is the budget. The budget process will put you squarely in front of your CFO. And he or she has a few questions…

CALL LOAD VS. PAID HOURS

If this issue hasn't come up yet, it will. Why is the annual call load so low vis-a-vis the call center's total annual paid hours? (These kinds of tough questions help explain why CFOs get the big bucks.) Some quick pencil work proves the point:

1. 790,000 annual calls X 3.5 minutes average handle time = 2,765,000 minutes
2. 2,765,000/60 = 46,083 hours, annual call load
3. 55 Full Time Equivalents (FTEs) = 114,400 annual paid hours (55 X 2,080 hours)*
4. 46,083/114,400 = 40 percent

*Assumptions: one year = 260 work days or 2,080 hours, based on eight-hour days. The call load and FTE figures are examples only.

Hmm… Why are you call center people spending so little time — 40 percent of aggregate paid hours — actually handling calls? Isn't that what you're here to do?

Of course, the first thing to ensure is that all of the responsibilities that fall under the call center's umbrella are included in the calculation. Are the loads associated with handling e-mail transactions, postal mail, outbound calls and other types of work sufficiently accounted for? Fair enough. Even so, the number is still likely to appear low, usually well under 50 percent Why? This discussion often leads to a more specific look at how individuals spend their time.

Chapter 4

OVERALL SHRINKAGE

Vacation/sickness	20 days	7.69%
Breaks	two 15 minute breaks	6.25%
Training	15 days	5.77%
Meetings	30 minutes per week	1.25%
Holidays	7 days/year	2.69%
Miscellaneous	20 minutes/day	4.17%
Total		**27.82%**

If you break down an individual's paid hours across a year, it might look something like the example in the table below.

Now that looks much better. If the time agents spend away from the workload amounts to around 28 percent, then they ought to be available to handle transactions 72 percent of the time. But why the dichotomy between this perspective and the 40 percent derived from the previous example? It is, in short, an "apples to oranges" comparison.

For one thing, those with supporting roles, who generally spend little of their time handling transactions, are omitted from the calculation. It takes a proverbial small army of trainers, technicians, analysts and supervisors to keep a call center humming along.

Another critical factor being ignored is the impact of occupancy. Occupancy is the percent of time that agents who are handling transactions are either in talk time or after-call work (wrap-up). The inverse of occupancy is the time agents spend waiting for calls, plugged in and available. Occupancy is inversely related to service level; when service level improves, agents will spend more of their time waiting for calls to arrive. This is an immutable law stemming from the phenomenon of random call arrival. Want to provide a good service level? Your "efficiency" will inherently be lower. The size of agent groups also affects occupancy; small groups are inherently less efficient than larger groups.

There may also be questions around schedule adherence and whether the factors included realistically reflect the activities that keep agents from the phones. The time spent on training, off-line research and miscellaneous projects has a tendency to expand over time. However, don't draw quick conclusions without a closer look; some or most of this time may necessarily reflect the growing responsibilities of today's call centers. There is also a danger in utilizing aggregate shrinkage in budget calculations, given that the things which keep agents off the phone vary by time of day, day of week and season of the year. The analysis will have to be more specific.

But perhaps the toughest issue to come to grips with revolves around scheduling accuracy and flexibility. Inbound call centers inherently operate in a "demand-chasing" mode. Much of the time, there are either more calls to be answered than resources available, or more resources than calls. Because supply and demand are rarely equal, demand must be "chased" with the supply of answering capabilities. The tough question is, what level of "insurance" do you want to build into your staffing calculations for those times when your forecasts and plans are off the mark or when schedules are not flexible enough to sufficiently respond to peaks and valleys in the workload?

When considering this issue, remember two caveats:

1. Budget projections usually assume ideal schedules with just the right number of base staff to handle the anticipated workload, plus expected shrinkage. Although it's tough to admit that your projections may not always be on the mark, you will need to build some worst-case scenarios to draw adequate attention to this question.

2. Unlike most other work environments, inbound call centers can't stockpile finished calls (work ahead) or handle unfinished calls in batch at a later time (catch up). The resources have to be in place when the work arrives, or we risk the consequences of angry callers, stressed agents and the high costs associated with long queues.

EDUCATE AT THE EXECUTIVE LEVEL

The bottom line... er, crux of the matter is that we need to be able to dialog intelligently and thoroughly on these issues. The CFO has a right to ask tough questions and to assess how wisely we're using the budget they're entrusting to our stewardship. But they are going to need at least a basic understanding of call center dynamics in order to understand the numbers. We have the responsibility of educating them on this unique environment and providing analysis that accurately reflects call center activities. If we don't, we're likely to end up with an inadequate budget.

The budget process also invariably leads to questions of strategy. For example, what is the call center's mission? How committed are we to providing good service even when the forecasts may be uncertain? What are our priorities, and how can we improve efficiency? What role will new technologies or processes serve and how will they impact the budget? Be ready for these discussions; they are opportunities for you to present thoughtful insight. This process is a healthy part of ongoing call center development.

Chapter 4

Calculating FTEs (Part 2): The Science and Judgment Behind FTE Budgets

by Brad Cleveland

Few call center management responsibilities require as much insight, know-how and collaboration as budgeting for full-time equivalents (FTEs). It is a multifaceted process laden with both "science" and "judgment." The steps based firmly on science tend to be the most straightforward (i.e., formulas, principles or immutable laws that yield predictable results). Those that require decisions around tradeoffs and unknowns tend to be more difficult and time-consuming.

Knowing where judgment comes in vs. the analysis best left to science is a challenge, but it's an important prerequisite to developing an appropriate budget. The following 10 steps summarize this process.

1. Analyze current results vs. stated objectives. What is the call center's mission? What are the supporting objectives? Are we meeting them? Why or why not? Was the budget from the last cycle appropriate? Did we forecast requirements accurately? What adjustments to the budget would we have made? Could we have better predicted outcomes? What can we learn this time around? This important first step includes some scientific analysis, but is largely based on business decisions.

Figure 1

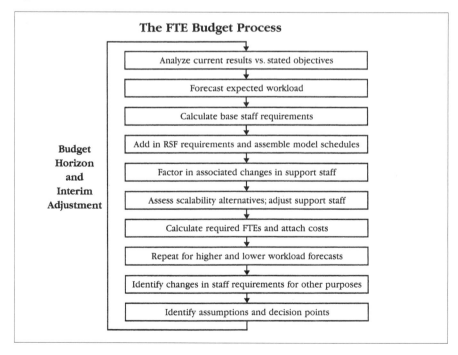

Figure 2

Leans toward "science"	Leans toward "business decisions"
 • Quantitative forecasting • Base staff calculations • Impact of "immutable laws" • RSF coverage • Schedule requirements • Accounting and cost analysis	 • SL and RT objectives • Agent group design • Judgmental forecasting • Contingencies/real-time plans • Schedule coverage rules • Schedule and budget horizons

2. Forecast expected workload. The principles of time-series forecasting (based on historical data), regression analysis (e.g., calls vs. new customers) and other types of quantitative forecasts are grounded in science. However, virtually all forecasts also require some judgment. For example, how will the call mix change as Web traffic grows? How should we structure agent groups (one crosstrained group requires one forecast, while many specialized groups require many specific forecasts)? What impact will changes in marketing, competitor activities, laws, consumer behavior and other developments have on the workload?

3. Calculate base staff and trunk requirements. Staff calculations are relatively straightforward and firmly based on science. Granted, all mathematical formulas or simulation models contain assumptions (e.g., what should we assume about busy signals and abandoned calls?). But the resources it will take to consistently achieve service level and response time objectives is a matter of mathematics.

4. Add in Rostered Staff Factor (RSF) requirements and assemble model schedules. RSF (also called an "overlay" or "shrink factor") leads to the minimum staff needed on schedule over and above base staff required. Although planning around issues such as schedule adherence and non-phone activities requires judgment, the RSF calculations themselves are straightforward and reliable. Defining schedule alternatives and coverage rules, on the other hand, tends to be more of an iterative, creative process.

5. Factor in associated changes in support staff. What should your staff-to-supervisor ratio be? How should the call center be organized? What analyst roles are necessary? This step depends more on observation, experience and good business sense than on science.

6. Assess scalability alternatives; adjust support staff. Scalability refers to the call center's ability to expand or contract without making changes in FTEs. For example, can other departments help to handle the load when the call center is busy? What other staffing contingencies are available? How committed is the organization to consistently meeting service level and quality objectives? These are business decisions.

7. Calculate required FTEs and attach costs. At this point, FTE and cost

Chapter 4

Figure 3

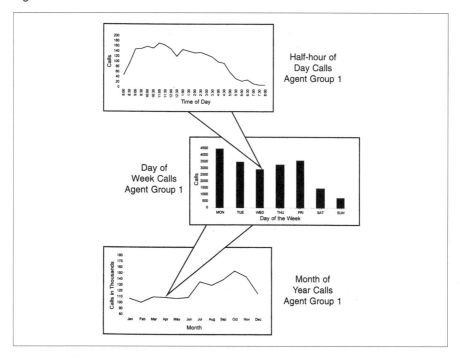

calculations are relatively straightforward. They are, of course, built on all of the assumptions that have come before.

8. Repeat for higher and lower workload forecasts. This step acknowledges any uncertainties in forecasts and is geared around different assumptions for workload.

9. Identify changes in staff requirements for other purposes. As in Step 5, identifying the needs for staff not directly associated with handling the workload is largely a matter of experience and observation.

10. Identify assumptions and decision points. In this final, critical step, you do an inventory of the assumptions made along the way. Not only will this impress the financial folks, it will create an efficient basis for discussing key issues and coming to agreements. Most importantly, it will increase everybody's understanding of key tradeoffs and improve the overall quality of the final budget.

NO MAGIC FORMULA

New managers often ask for "the formula" to calculate future FTE requirements. Sorry, there's no such thing. Instead, this is a process built on a combination of scientific calculations, business decisions and sound judgment. It depends on good communication and a solid understanding of the tradeoffs. And it requires that every decision-maker have a good understanding of what makes call centers tick.

Chapter 5:
Improving Real-time Collaboration and Management

Call Center Professionals Speak Out
on the Power Struggles Behind Forecasting and Scheduling

Focused Service Level Management

Striving to Meet Service Level 'Real-time'? Don't Ignore These Principles

Call Center Professionals Speak Out on the Power Struggles Behind Forecasting and Scheduling

by Greg Levin

Despite use of the latest workforce management software, many managers in charge of forecasting and scheduling at their call centers struggle to accomplish what they were hired to do. It's not due to a lack of effort or knowledge on their part, they say. Rather it's the lack of authority and support given to them by upper management, who, the managers say, don't truly understand the intricacies of forecasting and scheduling or the call center operation as a whole.

"My senior managers understand that forecasting needs to be done, but they don't understand all the variables that drive the amount of people we need to schedule to achieve our service level objectives," says a manager of a large call center in the financial services industry who requested anonymity. "I often make sound staffing suggestions that are rejected because management claims something like, 'We never had to do that before.'"

Senior managers often ignore the findings and suggestions of the forecaster, agrees Kathleen Peterson, CEO of Powerhouse Training Consultants, but she points out that, in some cases, senior management isn't supportive because the forecaster may have done a poor job of explaining findings to management in the past.

"Some forecasters don't do a good job of communicating the numbers to management or of making a compelling case, so their seniors managers may be wary of making requested staffing changes or increases," says Peterson.

But the reason some call center forecasters aren't able to make their cases regarding staffing needs, she adds, points back to their original complaint — their position is viewed by management as a low-level one. "Call center forecasters are often viewed merely as back-room analysts. The challenge is to leverage their position with senior managers to have the information they provide taken seriously."

SCHEDULES OFTEN OVERRIDDEN AT INSURANCE CALL CENTER

"Upper management looks at us as if we are merely data-entry people," says an anonymous manager in charge of forecasting and scheduling for an insurance call center. "That really short-changes what we do."

Reps at her call center have a lot of off-phone responsibilities, such as written correspondence and other projects, so accurate forecasting is necessary to determine when reps can complete these tasks without disrupting service levels, she explains. She has the tools she needs for effective forecasting, but not the authority to carry out her scheduling plans.

"I use TCS workforce management software, which does an excellent job in helping me decide how many people we need on the phones at particular times based on historical data. But my scheduling suggestions are often overridden. A prime example occurred just the other day: I got a memo from the Human Resources department telling me that they decided to randomly schedule people with less than a day's notice. This meant that I had to accommodate whatever they felt was necessary. They just don't always understand the scope, purpose and benefits of what forecasting and scheduling can do for them."

The common view of the call center as a mere backroom operation leads to another problem that has a negative effect on forecasting — lack of communication from the marketing department.

She also often has to lock horns with people in the financial department to get her schedules accepted. "They'll tell me, 'You should really only have X number of heads staffed for this period.' And I'll tell them, 'You really need to look at it from the standpoint of how many reps we need to maintain coverage and achieve service levels.'"

She often reminds upper management that she is using a very intricate and capable TCS system to assist her in her job, but says that these words often fall on deaf ears. "I've explained how I've come up with my schedules, how I've arrived at the numbers, but my schedules continue to be changed or watered down. I just wish that headcount in our call center was based on what the workforce management software says, not the bean counters. Sometimes I wonder why the company even bothered to invest in [the TCS system]."

MANAGER CLAIMS SENIOR MANAGEMENT
TOO RIGID TO EXPLORE OPTIONS

One call center manager in the automobile industry claims that her senior management doesn't stand behind the notion of flexible scheduling. "In the call center environment, we need a flexible workforce, but management doesn't want to enforce that," she explains. "They feel it's easier to have reps on a fixed schedule."

She points out that her reps prefer the fixed schedules and, because her call center is located in a region where unemployment is low, management feels it has to appease reps to keep them from looking for work elsewhere. "The philosophy [of management] is, 'Let's get them in the door, give them a nice fixed schedule, and they'll at least fill some of our staffing needs. We may have a shortage here or an overage there, but at least we'll have some warm bodies handling calls.'" She acknowledges that the low unemployment situation does minimize the staffing options, but that the company needs to make an attempt at creating a more flexible workforce.

Chapter 5

The manager says she constantly offers scheduling suggestions based on her forecasts to help fill foreseen gaps in staffing, but that those suggestions are rarely considered. "It's frustrating because I know in advance that we are going to have a hole in staffing. I'll let senior management know about it, but few steps will be taken to fill that anticipated hole."

Contributing to senior management's rigid scheduling practices is the fact that the call center's former workforce management software did not fit the center's needs. The software package was not compatible with the systems the call center was using, resulting in "some funky numbers," says the manager. The software package has since been vastly improved, but the damage has been done, she explains. "When you start off with one workforce management tool that doesn't work well, people begin to doubt every forecast you produce thereafter."

The manager says the forecasts that she now comes up with using the revamped workforce management software are usually accurate, but that she is unable to act on these findings because of the skepticism and lack of support from upper management.

LACK OF FORECASTING EXPERTISE, COMMUNICATION HINDER SUPPORT, CONSULTANT SAYS

Consultant Peterson understands these call center forecasters' frustrations and has seen firsthand how management often fails to recognize the value of the forecasters' work. She suggests that those in charge of forecasting and scheduling closely evaluate the work they are doing and how they communicate their findings to upper management. "Before beating up the big guys, [the forecasters] need to take a good look at how they are coming up with their numbers and how they are presenting their case. Whether it's a small, medium or large call center, I think it's the exception that the person in charge of forecasting and scheduling is an expert who is able to clearly justify suggested staffing needs."

Forecasters need to realize that what a call center is and how it functions is still not fully understood by those who don't work in them each day, she adds. Therefore, it is essential to have somebody — either the forecaster or another member of the call center — who has a strong relationship with the senior managers, who can get them to listen and understand the forecasting and scheduling process.

The forecasters interviewed all say they try to educate senior management, but that their efforts are thwarted because management views them as backroom number-crunchers. "I do a lot of detailed explaining and give out a lot of information, but I get little response," says the manager of the insurance call center.

The common view of the call center as a mere backroom operation leads to another problem that has a negative effect on forecasting — the lack of communication from the marketing department. The manager of the automobile call center says she works hard to input accurate numbers based on historical data when calculating staffing needs for a particular period, only to find out later that Marketing sent out a promotion without informing the call center.

Forecasters need to realize that what a call center is and how it functions is still not fully understood by those who don't work in them each day.

This leads to unexpected increases in call volume and damages her credibility as a good forecaster. "It's like pulling teeth trying to get the information I need from [the marketing department]," she says.

Forecasters need to take an active role in gathering information from departments such as Marketing, says Peterson, rather than wait for those departments to come to them. "Instead of complaining about being left out of the loop, those in charge of forecasting in the call center need to do everything they can to make sure they are included in the loop. They need to interact with the Marketing folks and find out what's coming down the pike."

Todd Tanner, senior consultant for the Tanner Group, agrees that forecasters and call center managers, in general, need to battle for respect, but acknowledges that it can be a difficult fight. "I have found that the higher you go in an organization, the more detached the people are from the operations of the call center," Tanner explains. "Because they are often so detached from the call center, upper management often discounts many of the tools — including workforce management tools and Erlang C — used to help the call center operate better."

Tanner agrees that forecasters sometimes do a poor job of explaining how they arrived at their numbers and of cost-justifying their staffing suggestions. But he also feels that most senior managers would struggle to understand the process even if the information was presented more clearly. It's not that senior managers are stupid, he explains, but that most of them are too distant from the call center to comprehend the intricacies of forecasting and scheduling.

ACTION REQUIRED BY BOTH PARTIES
TO MAXIMIZE VALUE OF FORECASTING

So what's the solution? According to Tanner, two things need to occur before call center forecasters will receive the support they need from senior management to do their job effectively. "First, those in charge of forecasting and scheduling need to become complete experts at what they do. They need to learn how to better use historical data and workforce management tools and, more importantly, be able to justify their findings."

But the forecaster's efforts will be wasted unless senior management gets into the game, he adds. "Senior management has to evolve, to make an effort to understand the call center environment." This entails going to a call center seminar or conference to learn the basics of forecasting and scheduling, Tanner explains. "They need to realize that by taking the time to learn how it all comes together, they will be able to help turn the call center into a profit center."

Chapter 5

Focused Service Level Management

by Gerry Barber

The ability to react to call volumes in real time determines the success of your call center. Making good resource and call-flow decisions on the fly will help you to attain consistent service levels. You can spend all the time you like mulling over yesterday's reports, but you can't do anything to recover lost payroll dollars or the customer dissatisfaction of yesterday. You need to focus on "what's happening now" to achieve consistent results. This brings us to an important technique than can help your call center to succeed — focused service level management.

Focused service level management is the art of utilizing your staff to attain the best service level at the lowest possible cost. A critical element of focused service level management is the introduction of a service level coordinator to the call center. The service level coordinator's primary responsibility is executing service level action plans — daily plans that describe what needs to be done in terms of staffing and call routing in a variety of call center situations. Having one person/group focusing on these issues will enable other managers and supervisors to spend more time assisting reps and focusing on serious customer issues.

I suggest that call centers with more than 30 seats or 1,500 calls per day deploy at least one dedicated coordinator. More coordinators may be required in a larger center or one that has extended business hours of operation. The coordinator should report to the highest level manager in the call center. (See figure 1, page 87, for a typical job description for a service level coordinator.)

THE ACTION PLAN

Service level coordinators can't be effective without established service level action plans. Everyone in the call center needs to be aware of the various plans, including how and when they are to be executed. Action plans that are poorly communicated will fall short.

Coordinators should focus on the following steps when creating a service level action plan:

• **Establish service level goals.** Determine an acceptable service level range that fits your organization, such as: "Our target service level is to handle 90 percent of all calls within 15 seconds, with over 75 percent answered with an acceptable range of 85 percent to 92 percent in 15 seconds." The appropriate action plan is implemented when the call center service level is above the range or below the range.

• **Create a rolling forecast of calls report.** Compare your call forecast against the original forecast every 15 minutes and make any necessary staffing decisions based on the finding. Many manpower-planning software packages have reports that are helpful in this area.

• **Create a scheduling adherence reporting system.** Because it's so important to have the right personnel in place at the right time, make sure that start, break, training and end-of-shift times are kept on schedule. Again, software is available to accomplish this with speed and accuracy.

• **Keep up-to-date employee databases.** A most important database is the home telephone list. Develop an "on-call" program by listing the extra hours and days employees are willing to work. Maintain a database of former department members who have moved to other jobs that can help in an emergency. Also, develop a job cross-reference chart that lists all the capabilities of your staff. The more you know about who can do what, the faster you can execute contingency plans.

• **Install a telephone system that can provide real-time information.** Most ACDs and PBXs provide some real-time information, such as number of calls in queue, agent status and service level. Seek systems that enable greater

Figure 1

Job Description: Service Level Coordinator

PRINCIPLE RESPONSIBILITIES:

- Develops action plans to handle unexpected call surges and/or to reduce staff during off-peak call times. Executes these plans in real time during appropriate situations.
- Supervises forecasting and scheduling for the entire call center to meet service level and cost-containment objectives.
- Provides hourly, daily, weekly and monthly reports on all aspects of the call center's performance.
- Maintains employee databases, job cross-reference information and on-call status lists.
- Coordinates and communicates all telephone equipment needs, including ACD system and call-routing changes, to corporate telecommunications department.
- Supervises, trains and evaluates service level team staff, who assist the coordinator in his or her responsibilities.

JOB QUALIFICATIONS:

A working knowledge of call center operations and job functions, prior experience with ACD systems, and some experience with telephone moves and changes. A minimum of three years' call center experience — with at least two years in a supervisory position — is preferred. Must be PC proficient and be able to maintain databases and use spreadsheet reporting systems. Must be able to react quickly and make decisions in real time, and to communicate and work well with individuals at all levels of the organization.

Chapter 5

user flexibility, such as the ability to design Windows screens that show call center information the way you want it.

• **Establish an open-shift posting program.** When preplanned absences occur, post those hours for others to take. When you're reforecasting call volumes and labor needs, and you find that there is a need for agents to take additional hours, post notification. When you need people to take time off, post it. Make the flexibility available through open-shift posting an employee benefit and make sure all personnel understand the posting rules.

The plan of action should also contain policy and procedures for the following issues:

• **Calling in off-duty reps.** Identify what events will trigger calling in additional personnel and how the process will be carried out.

• **Sharing personnel between activities.** The service level coordinator needs to know who they can re-deploy, the effect it will have on the department, who will share employees and the outer limits (percent of help) that can be safely taken from other activities.

• **Identifying when senior management is to be informed of problems.** Criteria needs to be established to notify senior management of the need for greater assistance or alternative actions.

• **Implementing special call-routing procedures.** This may include adding automated technology to assist callers, special delay messages, call-back messaging or changes in call routing in and outside of the center.

• **Deploying supervisors and managers on the phones.** Occasionally, heavy call volumes require the aid of supervisors and managers to help out on the phones. Establish clear guidelines on how and under what circumstances this process should be carried out. Clear communication saves valuable time in situations where quick implementation is essential.

COORDINATING SERVICE

Remember, a poor service level during the current period affects the next period and so on. Service level coordinators who focus on reducing delays now will reduce the number of calls from spilling over into the next 15- or 30-minute service level measuring period. Thus, there will also be fewer customer abandons and callbacks. During slower times, the service level coordinator should be looking for ways to re-deploy and reduce payroll. There's no need to achieve a 100 percent service level when an 80 percent service level fits the budget and is appropriate for your calling customers.

Striving to Meet Service Level 'Real-time'? Don't Ignore These Principles

by Brad Cleveland

An important challenge in running a call center is ensuring that everybody, especially supervisors and reps, have a basic understanding of key principles of call center planning and operation. I'm convinced that everything works better when the troops know what's behind things like service level, quality, scheduling and the pace of the center.

A part of this challenge is to clear up some misconceptions that may exist. For example, staff may see little connection between what they do and what those in planning roles do. They may feel like they have different, perhaps even competing objectives. The following points address some of the common misunderstandings in the area of real-time management. Take the time to clarify these issues with your staff. The effort will be well worth it.

SERVICE LEVEL IS NOT A REAL-TIME REPORT

Service level, as reported on past half-hours, hours or days, is historical data. So is service level, as reported "real-time" on readerboards or supervisor monitors. The ACD system has to look back some number of calls (i.e., 50) or some amount of time (i.e., five minutes) in order to make the calculation. On the other hand, the number of calls presently in queue is a real-time report (i.e., "There are 17 calls in queue.").

Understanding this distinction explains apparent contradictions. For example service level can read 65 percent in 20 seconds, even though there are no calls in queue at the moment. Keep watching the monitor, though, and service level will begin to climb. Or service level may look high at the moment, even though an enormous amount of calls are stuck in queue. However, give it a few minutes and, unless circumstances change, it will be greatly reduced. In short, service level does not immediately reflect new developments.

For service level to make sense, supervisors must be trained to interpret it in light of the recent past and how many calls are currently in queue. The number of calls in queue should be the primary focus, since it foretells where service level is about to go (unless conditions change). Supervisors should then assess the state reps are in — signed off, auxiliary, handling calls, etc. — and make appropriate adjustments. If they focus only on service level, it may be too late to prevent a sizable traffic jam. To keep service level high, focus first on a more immediate indication of what's happening.

ADHERENCE TO SCHEDULE IS MORE THAN A QUESTION OF 'HOW MUCH'?

Many call centers track adherence factor, which is a measure of how much time reps spend plugged in, available to take calls. Often, it's viewed only as an

Chapter 5

issue of how much (i.e., "so and so had an adherence factor of 87 percent yesterday"). Equally important, though, is when during the course of the day reps are plugged in and available to take calls.

Two agent groups may have similar call loads, competencies, systems and the same adherence levels — say 90 percent — and get totally different service level results. In one group, reps don't adhere as well mid-morning when things are hectic, but they make up for it by being available much of the afternoon when the call load has quieted. In the other group, reps are plugged in when needed and do other activities as circumstances allow.

An important responsibility of supervisors and lead agents is to ensure that people are plugged in when they are most needed — as queues are building. They need to be equipped with real-time information and know what to look for. Those in the planning role need to measure not only how much time reps are available, but when they are available. Adherence is a two-part issue — when and how much.

> *An important responsibility of supervisors and lead agents is to ensure that people are plugged in when they are most needed: as queues are building.*

SERVICE LEVEL AND QUALITY MAY BE AT ODDS, BUT ONLY FOR THE MOMENT

I like to pose a simple question to groups with a mix of supervisors and planners: "Are quality and service level at odds with each other?" The typical answers intrigue me. Planners usually say something like: "No. If quality is not good, we'll be getting repeat calls and spending valuable time on waste and rework. That bogs down service level." Supervisors usually say: "Yes. They are at odd because we can rush through a lot of calls when the queue backs up, which will bring service level up. But we will be sacrificing quality to do so."

Both answers are correct; the difference is one of perspective. Supervisors tend to be focused on what's happening right now — and, for the most part, they should be. Those involved in planning tend to think about tomorrow, next week and beyond. In the short term, service level and quality are at odds. But over time, poor quality tends to negatively impact service level. So the emphasis must be on handling each call correctly, regardless of how backed up the queue is.

The problem is that supervisors and reps often believe they're getting mixed signals from management. "Hey, you train us to do a quality job, but then you put a lot of emphasis on service level. You put these queue displays in our faces, and get unhappy when service level drops. What do you really want?"

The answer: Both! Look at the calls in queue, make sure people are plugged in and in the right mode, and do what's possible to arrange non-phone activities around the call load as it arrives. But handle each call right the first time no matter what's happening with service level. That's not focusing on mutually exclusive objectives, but if your supervisors and reps believe it is, the issue needs clarification.

AN ACCURATE FORECAST IS EVERYBODY'S RESPONSIBILITY

A common perspective among those on the front lines is that the accuracy of the forecast depends entirely on the skills of those who do the forecast. Most reps and supervisors think of call volume when they think of forecasting. However, forecasting involves projecting out all three of the components of call load: average talk time, average after-call work and number of calls. Every rep has an impact on the components of call load and, therefore, on the data that will be used in predicting future call loads.

I recently visited an organization that made a concerted effort to find out why their call load forecast was so inaccurate much of the time. Service level was erratic throughout the day and week, telecommunications costs were unpredictable and schedules weren't matching staff with calls. Was it the unpredictable nature of calls or was there some aspect of forecasting that needed improvement?

This organization has two locations that are networked, requiring them to forecast and schedule for the aggregate call load. As part of their investigation, they graphed out average talk time and average after-call work, down to the half-hour level, for calls that ended up in each location. They discovered the average talk time pattern was consistent and similar in both sites, but that average after-call work time was erratic in one of the sites. The reps in that site did not have a clear understanding of what the mode was for and when to use it. Proper training of staff fixed the poor forecast at that site.

The emphasis must be on handling each call correctly, regardless of how backed up the queue is.

In a related example, another company was predicting handling times well, but was off the mark on volume. After some investigation, they identified transferred calls as the culprit.

Transferred calls are a necessary part of many call centers, but in this case, reps were inconsistent about when and why they would transfer calls — that was throwing off the forecast. Again, training was the answer.

So an accurate forecast is everybody's responsibility. And it's especially important to be aware of this in the context of real-time management: When those in the heat of the battle are understandably tempted to fudge a bit on data entry. The reality is, planners especially need accurate data for the busiest times.

DIFFERENT RESPONSIBILITIES, DIFFERENT PERSPECTIVES

People with different responsibilities often have different perspectives. That's unavoidable and, thank goodness, healthy. The challenge is to relay the message that each viewpoint complements what others are doing, and furthers the call center's objectives.

Chapter 5

Index

Publication Dates

How to Reach the Publisher

We would love to hear from you! How could this book be inproved? Has it been helpful? No comments are off limits! You can reach us at:

Mailing Address: *Call Center Management Review*
P.O. Box 6177
Annapolis, MD 21401

Telephone: 410-267-0700, 800-672-6177

Fax: 410-267-0962

E-mail: icmi@incoming.com

Website: www.ccmreview.com

About Incoming Calls
Management Institute
and Call Center Press, a division of ICMI

Incoming Calls Management Institute (ICMI) offers the most comprehensive training programs and educational resources available for call center management professionals. Established in 1985 and the first to offer training on call center management, ICMI is a global leader in call center management training, publications and consulting.

ICMI's focus is helping individuals and organizations understand the dynamics of call center management in order to improve operational performance and achieve business results. ICMI provides high-caliber education and consulting to organizations ranging from small, start-up firms to national governments to multinational corporations.

Call Center Press, a division of ICMI, publishes the authoritative journal *Call Center Management Review* and the popular "how-to" book for call center managers, *Call Center Management On Fast Forward*.

A recognized pioneer in the field of call center management, ICMI is independent and not associated with, owned or subsidized by any industry supplier.

Visit www.incoming.com for more information on ICMI, industry resources, research and links, and to join a network of call center management professionals.

CONTACT INFORMATION:

Mailing Address: P.O. Box 6177
Annapolis, MD 21401

Telephone: 410-267-0700, 800-672-6177

E-mail: icmi@incoming.com

Website: www.incoming.com (ICMI)

www.ccmreview.com (*Call Center Management Review*)

Author Biographies

Gerry Barber is senior vice president at WebHV Solutions in Nashville, Tennessee. He is well-known for his strategy of blending the right technology with people, work procedures and empowerment policies, and is recognized as a leader in the strategic use of call center technology.

Brad Cleveland is president of Incoming Calls Management Institute and is publisher of *CCMReview*. He has advised organizations across five continents and has written numerous articles on the call center industry for business and trade publications. He is also co-author of *Call Center Management on Fast Forward: Succeeding in Today's Dynamic Inbound Environment*.

Henry Dortmans is president of Angus Dortmans Associates – a Toronto-based management consulting firm specializing in call centers and telecommunications. He is a Certified Associate of Incoming Calls Management Institute (ICMI) and has led ICMI seminars for organizations across Canada.

Greg Levin is the former editor of *Call Center Management Review* and author of the In Your Ear call center humor series. Greg is currently a freelance writer based in Spain.

Gordon Mac Pherson, now retired from the call center industry, founded both *Call Center Management Review* (formerly *Service Level Newsletter*) and Incoming Calls Management Institute (ICMI). For his early industry contributions to inbound call center management education and development, he was honored with the Call Center Pioneer Award 2000 from *Call Center Magazine*.

Ann Smith is president of Dallas-based A.G. Smith Consulting and Training, an independent consulting firm specializing in call center management. She is a Certified Associate of Incoming Calls Management Institute (ICMI), and has delivered ICMI seminars throughout North America and Europe.

Order Form

QTY.	ITEM	PRICE
	Call Center Forecasting and Scheduling: The Best of Call Center Management Review – 104 pages, paperback, more than 35 charts and graphs – $16.95 each* *Multiple Publicaion Sales Discount	
	Call Center Management On Fast Forward Book – 281 pages, paperback, more than 100 charts and graphs – $34.95 each* *Multiple Publicaion Sales Discount	
	Call Center Management On Fast Forward Book on Tape – $49.95 each	
	Call Center Management Review – monthly 20 page journal $337 (1 year subscription)	
	CD-ROM Tools for Incoming Call Center Managers – $49.00 each**	
	Shipping & Handling @ $5.00 per US shipment plus $1.00 per book/tape set and $.50 per software order. Additional charges apply to shipments outside the US.	
	Tax (5% MD and 7% GST Canada)	
	Total in U.S. Dollars	

*11-20 Copies (10% off) • 21-50 Copies (20% off) • 50+ Copies (30% off)

**CD-ROM includes software with the Erlang C and Erlang B formulas to calculate staff, occupancy, trunk load, service level, average speed of answer and calls in queue, as well as other software tools.

☐ Yes, please send me a free issue of *Call Center Management Review* and information on other publications and seminars.

Please ship my order and/or information to:

Name _____

Title _____Industry _____

Company _____

Address _____

City _____State_____Postal Code _____

Telephone (   ) _____Fax (   )_____

E-Mail _____

Method of Payment (Check one)

☐ Check enclosed (Make payable to ICMI Inc.; U.S. Dollars only)

☐ Invoice me

☐ Charge to: ☐ American Express   ☐ MasterCard   ☐ Visa

Account No. _____Expiration Date _____

Name on Card_____

Fax order to: 410-267-0962
call us at: 800-672-6177 (410-267-0700)
order online at: www.incoming.com
or mail order to: ICMI Inc.
P.O. Box 6177, Annapolis, MD 21401